MEMOIRS OF EUGENIE SCHUMANN

ROBERT SCHUMANN AND CLARA SCHUMANN
IN THE YEAR 1850 IN HAMBURG

From a daguerreotype in the Schumann Museum in Zwickau

THE SCHUMANNS
AND
JOHANNES BRAHMS

THE MEMOIRS OF
EUGENIE SCHUMANN

MUSIC BOOK SOCIETY
LAWRENCE, MASSACHUSETTS

First Published 1927

Reprinted 1991
from the original
provided by
The Public Library of
Haverhill, Massachusetts

International Standard Book Number
1-878156-01-2

PRINTED IN THE UNITED STATES OF AMERICA

DEDICATED TO MY SISTERS

MARIE AND ELISE

INTRODUCTION

WHEN I began to write down these Memoirs in the year 1920, I was guided by a definite intention. I find that erroneous statements are current concerning the lives and characters of my brothers. To disprove these by giving a faithful picture of their personalities as they are revealed first-hand in their letters, seemed to me a duty to them not only as beloved brothers, but as sons of our parents. I am not sure that I had publication in view ; I felt constrained to say how things had really been, and I started to write. One word led to another, one remembrance called forth a thousand. I wrote for the pleasure of writing ; I surveyed my life and lingered where I listed. The longer I wrote, the more it was my mother's personality which became the prominent one.

On her eightieth birthday I surprised my sister Marie with the first five chapters. She was pleased with them. A kind publisher who read them gave me encouragement, and induced me to supplement and revise. I took up the pen once more and found that I had many more things to say. The disconnected chapters became a book. If I have given little in it, it is the best that I have to give, the memories of great and good characters, of great and good times.

CONTENTS

LIST OF ILLUSTRATIONS

CHILDHOOD

I WAS born in Düsseldorf in December 1851, the seventh of eight children, boys and girls, and my father communicated the event to Grandmamma Bargiel in the following letter :—

' DEAR MAMMA !—You know what a letter from me usually means. Once more Heaven has protected Klara, and in the early hours of the morning a healthy child, a girl, was born. Fancy ! only three hours earlier Klara and I were present at the Jubilee party for Professor Schadow, which we did not want to miss. I am so happy that Klara is bright and well in spite of everything, and we will take great care of her during the next few weeks.

' Affectionate messages to your children, especially to Woldemar for the last things he sent me. I will write to him separately about that.

' We are preparing many musical events for the near future : a performance of the " Elijah," then Bach's Matthew Passion for the end of January, probably also of my fairy tale " The Pilgrimage of the Rose," the orchestration of which I have now finished. Perhaps Woldemar might come for that ? We must talk about it again.

' Now, affectionate greetings and kisses to yourself, and let us both thank Providence for having preserved our beloved Klara's strength. We hope to hear from you very soon.—Your   ROBERT.

' *Monday*, 1 *December* 1851,
  ' *At ten o'clock a.m.*'

Not the slightest remembrance of this dear father has remained with me ! No wonder, for in March 1854, when he was taken to Endenich, I was only two years and three months old. How often have I tried to penetrate the obscurity of the first years of infancy, always imagining that the form of him who must often have bent over my cradle would return to my consciousness ! But in vain ! The veil remained impenetrable. My birth was the last event he noted down in the ' Little Book of Memories ' which he kept for us children. I had resigned myself to the thought that it would remain the only visible sign of contact between him and me, when not long ago, to my unspeakable joy, I found in his letter to my mother dated April 1, 1855, these words : ' Write and tell me about Eugenie, she showed such quick intelligence.' So, after all, his thoughts had been occupied with me during his illness, as they had in times of health with my brothers and sisters.

His early death cast deep shadows on my life as well as on theirs. Even as a mere child I felt that I had sustained an irreparable loss. I thought of him continually, and shed many tears over the sad fate which had overtaken him. Later, I tried to picture his personality to myself, tried to imagine what it would be like to have a father. But I did not succeed ; all that I was told about him did not make him a living person. As I grew up I learnt to love him in his works. Modest as my musical gifts were, they were sufficient to make me apprehend his spirit. I felt deeply the fervour, the devotion and purity of his nature ; the high aspirations of his soul, the wonderful wealth of ideas. In imagination I re-created him and the psychic processes which had led to his sad fate. Once, when I was lying dangerously ill, I said to my doctor : ' I do not wonder at my father's illness, because no end of flowers were blossoming in his head.'

Nor have I many remembrances of my mother from the early years of my childhood. The first is from the Düsseldorf years. We younger children were playing together in the dining-room one evening, when it suddenly

2

occurred to us : We will go in to Mamma, she will give us chocolates. But we had first to cross another room, to our childish imagination enormous, with a stand in one corner, on which hung a large yellow fur coat that my father had worn on his trip to Russia. We dreaded this fur coat like a wild animal, and needed all our courage to pass it. We took one another by the hands, bolted through the darkness and burst into Mamma's room. There she was, sitting at her writing-desk by the light of a bright lamp. I can still see her, her slender form dressed in a black velvet bodice and silk skirt. How safe we felt after the danger we had braved ! She kept us with her for a little while, took the coveted sweets out of a drawer of her desk, and sent us away again.

My second recollection dates from the year 1857, when I was five years and six months old. I see my mother standing in the water and holding out her arms to me ; some one lifts me up, and she takes me and dips me into the stream. That was at St. Goarshausen, and my mother had bathed me in the waves of the Rhine, given me baptism for life, for I feel certain that this moment, inseparably bound up with the image of my mother, has inspired me with that passionate love for the Rhine which has accompanied me through life ; love for our German Rhine, our child of sorrows, for whose sake much blood has been shed, and still more will be shed in the future.

Another incident which I remember in connection with this stay in St. Goarshausen is an excursion to the ' Loreley ' rock, when the young woman in charge of us was dissolved in tears. I did not know the cause of her sorrow, and had I known it I should probably not have understood it. But from that day the ideas of ' Loreley ' and tears have always been connected in my mind.

In the year 1858 we spent a few weeks in Göttingen, and I remember my mother in a white muslin dress with black sprigs and a broad black sash, playing hide-and-seek with my elder sisters and our friends Brahms, Grimm, and Agathe Siebold. She had hidden in the thick green of an asparagus bed. Chased out of it, she ran as fast as she could towards the tree which was ' home,' and I have never forgotten the shock when, close to it, she stumbled over a root and fell headlong.

Yet another incident from those years has remained so firmly imprinted on my memory throughout all my life, that, although it is not connected with my mother, I cannot resist describing it. I see, as though it were in a picture, a group of children standing in the hall of our house in Düsseldorf. With amazement and admiration they are looking up at the banisters, on which a fair young man is performing the most daring gymnastics. He hoists himself from right to left and up and down ; at last he raises himself firmly on his arms, with his legs high in the air, and a final leap lands him below in the midst of the admiring crowd of children. I and my elder brothers and sisters were the children, and the young man was Johannes Brahms.

A few months after my father's illness had declared itself, the necessity of earning money became urgent for my mother ; she had to make up her mind to lead an itinerant life, and to leave the care and education of her children to strangers. Marie and Elise, Ludwig and Ferdinand, were sent to school, Julie to live with Grand-mamma Bargiel, and only Felix and I remained at home. At first we were in Düsseldorf in the care of a trustworthy person ; later on in Berlin under that of our sisters, who had the help and advice of a friend of our parents, Fräulein Elisabeth Werner, whom we called ' Aunt Elisabeth.'

The move to Berlin took place in the year 1857. A beautiful flat had been taken, a feature of which was of course the so-called Berlin central room, with one large window opening into the court. We little ones lived in this room, which had a south aspect. Here also stood the

4

old-fashioned square piano for our practice, while our sisters used the beautiful grand in the front drawing-room. Sometimes Marie would be with us, sometimes my second sister Elise, occasionally both together. An unforgettable little scene is connected with one such occasion, at which I was a petrified spectator. Elise, who was often depressed and moody during those years, leant at the open window and looked fixedly down into the Schöneberger Quay. She had beautiful long fair hair, which she wore in plaits pinned up with innumerable hairpins. Marie said something to her and got no answer. Incorrigible tease as she was, she tiptoed up to her sister, drew out one of her hairpins and threw it down into the street. Elise did not move. A second pin followed, a third, and in the end all of them. Elise had stood motionless all the time, but when the last pin was gone she turned round in a flash and administered a resounding smack to Marie's cheek.

Julie, too, must often have been with us. I have a vivid remembrance of a piano lesson with her, when she could not have been more than fifteen. She had just returned from our grandfather in Dresden, with whom she had been studying. At the beginning of my lesson she put a number of sweets, which had been given to her, on the lid of the piano, and promised me one for each well-played scale, study, etc. Every single exercise was declared a masterpiece, and the goodies were gone in no time, while many kisses were exchanged.

At night, when she had put us to bed, she took the candle and said, ' Now I am the woman who wants to blow out the candle,' and made a very wry mouth while she tried to blow. The light would not go out. Then she called, ' Husband, husband, come quickly and blow out the candle.' The man came ; he had his mouth awry the other way, and tried to blow, without success. Then ' Lieschen, Trude,' and so on, the daughters and the maid were called, but they all had wry mouths.

5

Julie was inexhaustible in the invention of an incredible variety of funny grimaces. Not one of the family was able to blow out the candle, and at last the night watchman, whose mouth was straight, was called in, and he blew it out. The light was gone ; a last little bit of fun, a last kiss in the dark from the dear girl, and she was gone.

We two little ones were inseparable. Felix was a child of so charming a disposition that he was everybody's favourite. I loved him so tenderly that I thought it only natural that he should be preferred to me. In December 1857, when he was three years and six months old, our uncle Woldemar Bargiel [1] wrote to our mother : ' Felix too is very lively, and has had a dream in which the Christ-child appeared to him in blue knickers and a blue coat, with a wreath on his head, and promised him a variety of presents. Caecilie will have to see to it that the Christ-child keeps his word. Felix is a splendid fellow.' Once he wished for a rocking-horse, but Mamma had earned so little in consequence of an accident that she could buy none of us Christmas presents. But Marie had a gold ring, which she sold, and Felix got his rocking-horse, on which I also was allowed to ride.

I remember our walks along the canal in winter, and the large tears which the bitter cold brought into my little brother's beautiful blue eyes. He had fur gloves, which hung suspended across his shoulders by a cord, but his little hands never remained long inside. Sometimes we were allowed to go on the apple-barges with our escort, where in oblong baskets apples of innumerable sorts were exhibited and sold by the fat apple-women.

I remember that we had to fold up the tablecloth after dinner, and how we would tug it out of each other's hands many times. I said, ' You are rude,' and Felix would reply, ' You are much rooter.' Once he pulled out one

[1] Woldemar Bargiel, half-brother to our mother. Caecilie, his sister.

ROBERT SCHUMANN
AS A YOUNG MAN
Artist unknown

of my teeth. We were playing ' horse ' ; I, as the coach-man, was sitting high up on a table placed on top of another ; my hands being otherwise occupied for the moment, I held the reins in my mouth. The horse started and the tooth was gone. Then again, I can see us sitting together for a whole day in an arbour of young branches, catkins, and rushes in the dining-room ; some one had probably built it for us on Palm Sunday. Once in May we were taken into a field where we found large brown beetles on a tree. We were told to shake the tree, and down came a great number of chocolate cockchafers. My tolerance for cockchafers dates from that experience ; otherwise all creepy and crawly things were an abomina-tion to me. In the summer we would often be taken to the Zoological Gardens, where we played ' Robbers and Soldiers ' or ' Wild Beasts ' all day on a large sand-heap with the Director's children.

We spent one summer with Mamma in Kreuznach, where we were taken on the River Nahe in rowing-boats. One scorchingly hot day Stockhausen was to be of the party. We were already seated in the boat when he came, attired in a large fur coat, declaring that that was the only sensible way of dressing in the summer, as nothing kept the heat off like fur. He was then giving several concerts with my mother, and sang the ' Müller-lieder ' among other things, singing himself for ever into my childish heart with his ' Ich hört' ein Bächlein rauschen.' The charm of this song as he sang it is unforgettable.

Marie likes to tell the story of a little fright into which Julie's passionate vivacity led her on the occasion of one of these concerts. The music-shop in Kreuznach where the tickets were to be sold, asked a percentage out of all proportion to the prices, so that our profits would have been much reduced. Marie and Elise therefore decided that they could quite well undertake the sale of the tickets themselves. My mother rather unwillingly

7

consented, and an advertisement was inserted in the local paper. Very soon the first applicants, two strange ladies, appeared. Julie rushed up to the elder sisters and begged fervently, ' Please, please, let me sell the tickets.' Before they could prevent her she had run past them into the room where they were sold. Marie and Elise, much annoyed, could do nothing but let things take their course. A few minutes later Julie returned, slowly, and evidently much upset. ' What has happened? Haven't they bought the tickets? ' ' Oh yes, the ladies bought two, but—but they haven't paid for them.' She was quite inconsolable, especially as the others treated it as a joke and laughed. The ladies soon sent the money, which they had probably hesitated to give to so youthful an agent.

It was during the years we were living in Berlin that a fortunate opportunity came to me which, although I did not realise it as such at the time, I have been glad to think of in later years. I saved the life of a little girl, and it came about like this. Herr and Frau Möllinger, with whom Felix and I were staying for a little while as boarders, had taken us into the country. We were playing with other children in a large farmyard. The centre of this was a small but deep pond with steep edge ; the water was black and muddy, full of croaking frogs. I do not remember exactly how it happened, but a little girl fell in and sank immediately, so that only her head and her small helpless hands could be seen. The others, younger than myself, ran towards the house screaming, but I did not hesitate a moment to climb down the steep edge and wade into the water as far as I could—perhaps I also had a stick handy : in short, I succeeded in pulling the child out. Meanwhile the people from the house came rushing towards us ; we were undressed and put to bed without delay. When next day Herr Möllinger gave me a beautiful doll and a new dress ' because I had been so brave,' I did not understand what he meant. It was not until much later that I realised how great was the danger from which I had saved the child.

I retain a vivid impression of my first meeting with our grandfather Wieck about this time ; after that I met him only once.   Probably he had invited Felix and me to stay with him in Dresden.   He was a tall, spare man with prominent features, and eyes of a deep blue, fiery eyes, and at the same time melancholy, such as are only found in Germans.   Other recollections of this visit do not extend beyond his giving us money to spend in amusements at the fair on the Vogelwiese, and his holding forth at great length one day to a number of people in the room, while Felix and I were sitting on the window-sill.   The peroration was : ' My Klara, my Klara, she is the best proof of what my method can produce.'

It is a curious fact that I have hardly any recollections of my mother during the years in Berlin.   I can understand it the less as I see from her diaries that she spent almost every Christmas with us, and that we were often with her during the summer as well.   Once, I remember, I was told, ' Go into the drawing-room ; you will find a surprise.'   When I went in, I saw with a feeling of indescribable happiness my mother lying down on a sofa, resting after a night journey.   I also seem to remember dimly that I often saw her crying.   But one thing I know for certain, that wherever she might be, we were ever conscious of her loving care, her protecting hold over us, and that to us little ones, as well as to the elder sisters and brothers, she was the greatest thing we possessed in the world.   As far as the enormous demands made by her profession would allow, she kept up our family life through her letters : she told us what the others were doing, begged us to write to each other, reminded us of each other's birthdays—in short, she did what she could to prevent estrangement between us.   We little ones had our share of letters, too, of which I give a selection :—

'KREUZNACH, 15 *September* 1860.

'MY DEAR EUGENIE,—Your little letter to me for my birthday has given me great pleasure—I hope you wrote it without help? You must always do that, then I can see what you can do by yourself and how much you have learnt. How are you getting on with your piano? Do you practise regularly for an hour every day? And do you cry now as you used to do? I hope not. We often talk of you here, and when I see a little girl or a boy I keep thinking it must be you and Felix. Well, if it is God's will, we will spend a few months together again next summer, but of course I shall expect you to have been ever so industrious.

'Write again very soon, my dear child, and always remember her who loves you tenderly, your

'MOTHER KLARA.'

To Felix.

'KREUZNACH, 15 *September* 1860.

'MY DEAR LIXEMÄNNCHEN,—That was a charming little letter which you sent me for my birthday! but I expect you did not write it by yourself? You must soon learn to do that. I am so glad that you have now got a violin. What is the name of the note which you played on it? G, D, A, or E? Be sure to write and tell me how many notes you can play. Soon perhaps there will be so many that you can no longer count them. Have you got a bag for putting your violin away? Be very careful of it, for a violin is not a toy. Now good-bye, you dear little fiddler. Be industrious and obedient, and often think of her who kisses you, your

'MOTHER KLARA.

'Give my kind regards to your master.'

CHILDHOOD

'Düsseldorf, 22 *December* 1860.

'My dear little ones,—On Christmas Eve when you are very happy, think of your Mamma, who would so love to be with you. To show you that I too am thinking of you, I am sending you these beautiful books, which you may read on Sundays if you have been very industrious during the week. But you must on no account spoil them or let them get dirty ; I should be very, very cross if you did ; they must always be kept nice.

'Are you doing your music really industriously ? Do you practise every day ? By yourselves, without help ?

'Now fare ever so well, my dear Eugenie and my dear Felix ; remember your mother very often, and be happy on Christmas Eve, and be good to dear Aunt Storch and Aunt Elisabeth. I kiss you in all motherly love and tenderness. Your

'Mother Klara.'

In the autumn of 1862 my mother bought a cottage in the village of Lichtenthal, near Baden-Baden. It had originally been a small farmhouse with large barn attached. A later occupant had turned the barn into several large living-rooms, and this gave a somewhat more residential air to the very modest exterior of the cottage. When approached from the main road of the village, it looked so plain and unattractive that we children had given it the name of 'the kennel.' Indeed, no one could at first sight believe that it was the home of an artist like my mother. When Hermann Levi, then conductor at the opera-house in Karlsruhe, called on her for the first time, we heard him say to the cabman, who had duly taken him to the address Lichtenthal 14 : 'No, this cannot be right ; Frau Schumann can't be living here.' And yet there she did live, and this same Hermann Levi and many friends and acquaintances, artists and royalties, have

11

spent delightful, inspiring, and enjoyable hours there. At that time the little town of Baden-Baden had quite a different character from its present one.[1] The Casino dominated the entire life of the place ; the distinguished and fashionable world of all countries, especially France, England, and Russia, congregated there, and the lessee of the Bank provided in the most lavish way for all the comforts and amusements which these foreign guests required. This was of great advantage to the inhabitants. The little town and its surroundings had an air of prosperity. Charming promenades delighted the eye ; to my mother the groups of deliciously scented azaleas were an ever fresh delight. The Kurhaus with its tastefully decorated halls, the concerts given by the excellent orchestra recruited from artists of the first rank, were open free to everybody ; and—rates and taxes did not exist.

In the spring of 1863 we moved in. I can still see the large furniture-vans standing in front of the ' kennel,' and Felix and myself sitting on packing-cases on the ground, making friends at once with the children from next door. My elder sisters took charge of the move, and my mother joined us a fortnight later. And now there began for us children a succession of the happiest summers of our lives. My mother used to be on tour during the winter months, mostly accompanied by Marie. We others were scattered about the world, and this modest but charmingly idyllic spot represented to us the paradise which united us all—some of us for the whole summer, some at least for the holidays. Here my mother could rest after her exacting winter campaigns ; here she belonged to us, lived for us and for our education and training, rejoicing when we had made progress during the winter, and feeling, alas ! only too anxious when everything had not gone as it should. Her love, her benevolence, order, industry, and her most faithful sense

---

[1] Baden-Baden was a famous gambling resort at the time.

of duty in things great and small, dominated the household. She divided the duties between us according to our capabilities, and kept a wholesome balance between work and recreation. When the weather was fine we breakfasted in the green trellised arbour of the garden, where we could enjoy the magnificent trees of the Lichtenthal Avenue, from which only the glittering, gently plashing little River Oos separated us. We could watch the people promenading up and down from our hiding-place; we saw the Queen of Prussia—afterwards the Empress Augusta—pass every morning, and in September the King, her husband, afterwards the Emperor William the First, would be seen walking by her side, with his truly royal bearing.

At breakfast-time letters were read and plans for the day made. My mother usually remained in the arbour for another hour, either writing letters or in conversation with her intimate friends, Fräulein Leser and Fräulein Jungé, who usually came to Baden for the whole summer, and were quartered near by.

We children then went indoors and attended to our various duties. The mornings were entirely devoted to work. From our earliest childhood we had all been trained in music, and practised in turn by the clock. My mother always impressed on us the importance of regular if not long practice. When Felix, as quite a little fellow, once asked her to let him off his practice, as it was a Sunday, she said to him : ' I should have been better pleased if you had asked me whether you might practise for two hours instead of one on a Sunday ; nevertheless, I will do what you ask.'

We had a beautiful grand for our practising, and at times there were as many as three grand pianos in the house, which different makers had sent to my mother. She, as our grandfather Wieck before her, was of opinion that a good touch could only be acquired on a grand, and I remember her being quite unhappy once when, later on, from want of room in a pension, I had to practise on an upright.

My elder sisters each had two lessons a week from Mamma ; we little ones were taught by our sisters, who were held responsible for our daily practices, even—and especially—during the holidays, much to my chagrin, for I did not at all like to be called off when I was playing in the garden or with the neighbour's children, Adolf, Elisabeth, and Flora Schwarz. I remember once clenching my fists at Elise, who was calling me over and over again, and repeating, ' I hate her, I hate her ! ' and Elisabeth, who was devoted to Elise, laughing and saying, ' And I love her, I love her ! '

As we were such a large family, there was always plenty to do. The lighter domestic work was done by my sisters. Marie managed the whole household ; she superintended kitchen and store-room, which was no easy matter, considering the number of people in the house and the constant coming and going of visitors. Besides this, she had the care of us little ones, our health, our clothes ; all this rested on her young shoulders. As far as I remember, I seldom wore as a child a dress which her clever fingers had not made. And she was not contented to make the things as simply as possible—they had to be pretty and in good taste. I see the materials before me now, which were mostly brought from England by my mother—white with red, white with blue, stripes, dots, sprigs. I can still feel the tension with which I watched the dress grow. Then, how great the excitement when the first sewing-machine came into the house, and the intricate marvel was explored ! My mother's wardrobe also had to be seen to, shopping to be done, while Marie's own musical education could not be neglected. And she did all these things without fuss, quietly and cheerfully, expecting no appreciation of any kind. My childish mind guessed, even in those early years, that this eldest sister was a treasure to Mamma, to us all ; but it was not until later, in my ripest years, that I fully understood her worth. I now look back with deep emotion upon this life, full of labour and care for those she loved.

Indeed, Providence had been kind to my mother in giving her the support of such a daughter. Thanks to Marie she could live entirely for her profession, untroubled by the onerous demands of everyday life, which were kept from her so as not to hinder her in the pursuit of her art, or bring her down from its heaven to solid earth. She could safely leave everything to Marie ; matters great and small were talked over with her, every plan made with her help. My mother fully repaid her devotion with tenderest love, to which gratitude gave a touch of pathos. Moreover, she insisted that ' Marusch,' as she then used to call her, should have due respect paid to her ; very early she gave her full independence, full power of action, and thereby made up to her for the sacrifice of her life. In later years, when I grew up and had my own ideas about the management of domestic affairs, I sometimes met with opposition from Marie ; but whenever I complained to Mamma that my views were not sufficiently considered, she used to say : ' You must never forget what Marie has been to me during the years after Papa's death, when you were all little things. I could not have lived through that time without her.'

In the afternoons we did needlework, and had coffee at four o'clock—we children in the dining-room, while Mamma received the many daily visitors in the drawing-room. In the later part of the afternoon we usually went for long walks, for which I did not care much during those years. I preferred to play with my friends. Moreover, Mamma was always very nervous ; when we ran on ahead or lingered behind, she thought we were lost, and was not happy until we were all gathered closely round her again. We were also strictly forbidden to walk along the edges of what Mamma called precipices, and that was,

of course, what we liked best. Later in life, when Mamma
was no longer able to walk so far, I have often longed for
these walks, when we would bring her every little straw-
berry, every pretty little flower. To our surprise she
would put them all into her pocket, saying they would
keep fresher there. We knew all her favourite spots.
How she enjoyed the dark pinewoods and the ' Freund-
liche Landschaft ' [1] beyond them ! One of her favourite
songs was my father's ' Sehnsucht nach der Waldgegend.' [2]
In her old age it still inspired her with all the enthusiasm
of youth. She did not avoid ' Verrufene Stellen ' [3] by any
means. Like all true Germans, she enjoyed feeling the
shivers run down her back. When she was young she
had preferred grand, even awe-inspiring scenery, but when
she grew older she was more attracted by a restful and
lovely landscape. Our walks usually included a meal at
an inn, which lent an additional charm to our walk ; and
Mamma's favourite dish, pancakes with a lot of sugar,
and lettuces with a lot of vinegar, was ours too. Then she
would tell us of the cucumber with vinegar which she
kept in her cupboard in the summer when she was a girl,
and ate from time to time to refresh herself during her
long hours of practising. Her appetite was always
excellent, and she liked her meals. She never found it
difficult to come down from the most exalted spheres and
attune her mind to physical comforts. I remember a
little story in reference to this. We were in Heidelberg
and had walked up to the Castle. The day was brilliantly fine, and Mamma was in a state of great enthusiasm
about the beauty of the ruins. On the terrace we met a
lady of our acquaintance, Frau W., with her family. We
all sat down at a table and ordered lunch. After we had
been kept waiting a long time, my mother at last said
impatiently, ' It is too bad of them to keep us waiting
like this.' Whereupon Frau W. sat up stiffly and spoke

[1] ' Charming Landscape ' from ' Waldscenen.'
[2] Songs, op. 35, No. 5.   [3] ' Haunted Spots ' from ' Waldscenen.'

16

CLARA WIECK
IN HER SEVENTEENTH YEAR

After a lithograph by T. Gare

the ever-memorable words, 'I cannot understand how one can think of prosaic things when Nature is providing such a magnificent feast.' Mamma only smiled, but we were furious, and never forgave the woman.

These were wonderful days, which now, on looking back, seem steeped in eternal sunshine. But the most wonderful of them was the day on which Mamma began to practise again after a fair interval of rest. Directly after breakfast the grand piano was opened and the house flooded with sound. Scales rolled and swelled like a tidal sea, legato and staccato ; in octaves, thirds, sixths, tenths, and double thirds ; sometimes in one hand only, while the other played accompanying chords. Then arpeggios of all kinds, octaves, shakes, everything prestissimo and without the slightest break, exquisite modulations leading from key to key. The most wonderful feature of this practising was that although the principle on which it was based was always the same, it was new every day, and seemed drawn ever fresh from a mysterious wellspring. Irresistible inspiration, perfect rhythm, such as springs from the souls of only the greatest artists, combined with absolute mastery of technique, made these exercises a wonderfully spiritualised achievement. A distant relative of ours, when she was staying with us, said that she had never believed the story told of Paganini, who made people weep with the playing of a scale ; but that now she had heard Mamma practise, she could understand it. I do not think any one could ever have forgotten it who had heard it, even once only ; and here were we children hearing it day by day. Though I was still so young, my mind was filled with inexpressible joy and satisfaction, and this has continued throughout my life, to the day when we heard it for the last time. We often pressed Mamma to write down the sequence of an hour's exercises, but she always said it was impossible to retain exactly this kind of free fantasia.

After the technical exercises, which, in those years, she always ended with Czerny's Toccata, came the turn of Bach : either the Italian Concerto, or several fugues from the Wohltemporierte Klavier, the great fugue in A minor, Chromatic Fantasia, the Organ Fugue in A minor arranged for piano by herself, and sometimes Partitas or Suites. Finally Schumann's Toccata and five or six studies by Chopin. She never practised in the sense usually attached to the word. I have never heard my mother practise slowly, bar by bar. She had overcome all technical difficulties when she was a child, and grown up with the new creations of Chopin, Mendelssohn, and Schumann, with those of Thalberg, Henselt, and Liszt. She had made herself acquainted with all these works immediately on their appearance. Now only those of Brahms were new to her, and to these she gave the right interpretation at first sight, without preliminary study. She penetrated so deeply into the spirit of each work, that they became almost part of her. They lay enshrined in her soul, and when she drew them forth they seemed to have been newly created. As a rule she practised without the music. I remember a few occasions when I came into the room while she was at work ; she asked me to find her the music in order to verify some point or other. We never disturbed Mamma without good cause when she was at the piano, but we knew that we might come in at any time, and that she even liked it. She always gave us a kind glance whenever we entered the room. I used to wonder at the time that she could go on playing so unconcernedly while she talked to us of other things. While she played scales she would often read letters open on the desk in front of her.

It was a sad time when autumn came. Mamma's birthday, September 13, the dearest festival of the year for us, also marked the end of our summer. Preparations for the winter then began. Mamma's wardrobe was overhauled, her large trunks were taken out, and

Marie performed the incredible ; she, when the hour of parting from the dear cottage came, was the saddest of us all.

She loved this home with all her heart, and in later years never got over our parting with it.

SCHOOL YEARS

IN the autumn of 1863 Felix was sent as a boarder to
Professor Planer in Berlin, who had already taken
charge of Ferdinand's education, and at the beginning of
October Marie took me to the large boarding-school
which Fräulein Marie Hillebrand kept in Rödelheim,
near Frankfurt a/Main. The school at that time enjoyed
a great reputation, and had been warmly recommended
to my mother by trustworthy friends. She was confident,
therefore, that I should be happy there. Marie stayed
with me for a few hours, and then left me to my companions, about a hundred girls of different ages. It had
no doubt been hard enough for me to leave Baden.
Since my earliest childhood it had been the first time that
I had stayed with my mother for several months in
succession ; I had seen all my brothers and sisters again,
and we had spent a most happy summer together. The
bitterness of a separation, presumably for many years,
was before me. I had been inseparable from Felix, too ;
now he and I were torn from each other. Was it not
natural that my tears should be flowing ? That on the
first day they should be flowing from early morning till
late at night ? In the evening I was standing in the
garden alone, the tears still streaming from my eyes.
Fräulein Hillebrand came towards me and said, ' Do
you know the fifth commandment ? If so, let me hear
it.' Obediently I stammered through the few words.
' Do you know that you are breaking this commandment ?
It is for your good that your mother has sent you here, and
now you keep on crying. Do you see how wicked that
is ? ' My tears ceased as if by magic, but at the same

time the doors of my heart were locked against this un-feeling woman, and were never opened again in the course of nearly three years which I spent under her roof. If she had taken into her arms this fatherless child of eleven, who was struggling against the first great sorrow in her life, and said, ' Eugenie, cry your fill, and then try to be cheerful again,' how different might have been our relations, how much more favourably might not my inner life have developed !

Fräulein Hillebrand belonged to a family of eminent scholars. Her father, Joseph Hillebrand, had been professor of philosophy in Heidelberg and Giessen ; he also had a reputation as a literary man. Her brother was the well-known Karl Hillebrand, who was implicated in the Baden rising in 1848 when he was only nineteen ; he fled to France in the following year and there found a second home, where he rose to a distinguished position as professor and author. We were told that Fräulein Hillebrand had helped in her brother's escape, not without danger to her own safety. She managed the whole school alone, almost without assistant teachers ; I can only remember a Mons. Roland who now and then gave us French lessons. Fräulein Hillebrand did not live with us in the castle, but in her private house beyond the park. She was nevertheless informed of everything, down to the smallest trifles, that passed at the castle. We pupils knew perfectly well that this was owing to a subtle spy system which she had instituted. We were divided into so-called ' parties,' groups of eight to twelve girls, but not according to our ages. Girls of ten were thrown apparently hap-hazard with those of eighteen and more. Each of these parties lived separate from the others, and only at meal-and lesson-times did we all meet. The special party of the ' disgraced ' was excluded from common meals, games, and walks. They appeared in the class-rooms after all the other parties had been assembled. Friendships were not tolerated ; as soon as two girls became friendly, they were separated. Once I and an older girl whom I particularly hated, constituted a party for months; we lived alone together from morning till night, and were sent for lonely walks. I was completely in her power. A certain number of pupils were under orders to report to Fräulein Hillebrand everything that happened and every word that was spoken. One of the elect, who happened to like me, once said to me : ' Schumännchen ' (we were all called by our family names), ' be careful what you say; I have to report everything.' I am proud to say that I never was one of the elect. Fräulein Hillebrand knew human nature too well to make such a mistake.

Our life was made a burden to us by these methods : we were denounced, we did not know by whom ; we were not given a fair trial, but ' simply punished.' When we cried out in the anguish of our soul, ' Why ? why ? ' we were told, ' You know perfectly well why.' Punishments were of a degrading kind, and left the mind in a state of depression long after they were done with. Later, when I read *Jane Eyre* and *David Copperfield*, I came to the conclusion that my experiences had not been very different from Jane's at Mr. Brocklehurst's or poor David's with his placard, ' Take care of him, he bites.'

So far as I remember, the food was bad ; anyhow, having been accustomed to the simple but well-prepared meals at home, I often felt a disgust for it, partly no doubt because it was served in tin basins on table-covers of brown oilcloth.

I have already mentioned that we were quartered in a castle. Fräulein Hillebrand had rented it from the proprietor, Count Solms-Rödelheim. It was mediæval, built of solid stone, and had several round towers. One of these towers, which was always locked, was credited with a ruined staircase and subterranean passages. Innumerable rooms were at our disposal, all of them lofty, bright, and airy. All the windows overlooked the spacious

park, the magnificent old trees and open places of which
made as beautiful a playground as one could desire. We
were not stinted in hours of recreation which we spent
there, and these were one of the few redeeming features
of our school life. The park was bordered on one side
by the yellow little River Nidda, a tributary of the Main.
One morning I saw Fräulein Hillebrand running up and
down there in great excitement. A young girl from
Frankfurt a/Main had disappeared during the night, and
Fräulein Hillebrand was looking for her footprints on the
banks. The fugitive was presently discovered at the
station of a small neighbouring place and, I believe,
brought back ; but she gave no peace until her parents
took her away from the school.

We had to take our full share of the domestic work, not
so much in the kitchen as in cleaning the bedrooms.
Being one of the younger ones, I was made to crawl under
the beds in a cotton frock to sweep the floor with a hand-
brush. I detested this work. Even during the coldest
winter months the dormitories were not warmed, and the
water which was put into the tin basins for us at night was
often solidly frozen in the morning. In winter we were
called at six, in summer at five. These early morning
hours during the weeks before Christmas are one of my
most dreadful recollections. When we left our icy-cold
dormitories, instead of going to our breakfast of milk and
water or thin acorn coffee, we were made to assemble in
the school hall. There was a fire, but it had not yet
sufficiently warmed the enormous room, which was also
badly lighted. We sat down ; Fräulein Hillebrand stood
on the platform with a devotional book in her hands. Her
dreaded features were thrown into full relief by the candle
in front of her, by the light of which she read out a long
passage. One of the pupils was called upon to repeat it
verbally without a mistake. Whenever my turn came,
there was a complete breakdown. I was quick in most
things, and had an excellent memory once I had grasped

the sense of anything, but what Fräulein Hillebrand read to us I did not understand. Perhaps it was too abstract, or I clung too anxiously to the words, dreading the impending examination. In short, I was always incapable of repeating a single one of these passages, and the hours of devotion which were intended as an uplift became a torture to me. I do not know what the book, chosen for this experiment, was ; but we put our heads together and decided it must be ' Roman Catholic.' This meant to us the quintessence of all that was incomprehensible and terrible.

There were, as I said, some redeeming features, notably the lessons, which, I know, I was even then capable of appreciating fully. To Fräulein Hillebrand the Alpha and Omega of all education was history. She devoted herself to it with enthusiasm, and had a genius for teaching it. She did not divide us into classes according to our ages for the lessons either, but assembled the whole school and opened the storehouse of her great knowledge ungrudgingly to us. Weber's *History* was our handbook. The different ' parties ' had to read up certain paragraphs of it ; the eldest girl of the party read them aloud, sentence by sentence, dictated notes, and examined on what she had read, so as to impress it on the memory. I still remember certain *clichés* from Weber which never failed to impress me, such as ' The people called for bread and the Church gave them a stone.' When all the parties were prepared, word was sent to Fräulein Hillebrand ; the bell soon summoned us, and from all over the house we poured into the hall, where we sat in trembling expectancy. I say ' trembling,' for Fräulein Hillebrand's demands in her lessons were as severe as in daily life. If a pupil had not completely mastered her difficult task she was doomed to punishment, the mildest being that you left the dinner-table after the soup with nothing but a piece of dry bread in your hand. Once Fräulein Hillebrand found us all insufficiently prepared, and this

ROBERT SCHUMANN

IN THE YEAR 1850 IN HAMBURG

After a daguerreotype hitherto unpublished, which was used by
Eduard Bendemann for his well-known drawing

punishment was extended to the whole school. When we had sat down to our frugal course, we found to our astonishment that the cook, who had already prepared the whole dinner, had put it bodily into the soup.

Before the lesson began, we thus sat in trembling expectancy, in wide ranks, pencil and copybook in our hands, until the door was opened and a small figure, dressed in black, softly glided into the hall. We sprang to attention, and more than one of us grew pale with excitement. Fräulein Hillebrand walked slowly to the platform; she mounted; her large, cold dark eyes glanced along the ranks, screwing like gimlets into one of the faces. 'Sit down,' she said, and the lesson began. One of the pupils was asked to recite what had been prepared, another continued at a sign from Fräulein Hillebrand, then a third, and so on. Questions pelted down upon us like hailstones at every turn, none knew when she would be hit. Not facts only—dates also had to be given without a moment's hesitation ; then we would be asked, ' What happened in Rome at that time, in Greece, in France, Germany, England ? ' Fräulein Hillebrand laid the greatest stress upon our surveying history as a whole, from primitive times to the present day. During the years of my sojourn in Rödelheim I believe I heard her go through the history of the world three times ; she correlated geography, science, and literature. What she then gave us was the best that she had to give. Her appeal as an orator was irresistible. On the subject of German culture and literature she kindled us to such enthusiasm that the impression has been fixed for ever in my mind. Though the time in Rödelheim was unhappy in every other respect for me, I have realised with gratitude that I owed this eminent woman something precious, something worth keeping for life. She not only gave me considerable knowledge as a basis for further study, but enabled me to grasp salient points and interrelations of things. Subjects other than history were

treated very perfunctorily ; we had no instruction at all
in writing and arithmetic, picked up a little French and
still less English. As far as I remember, we had lessons
in the mornings only ; the afternoons were taken up
with preparations for the next day's lessons, games in the
park, and long walks. In the summer we were sometimes
taken for excursions into the Taunus Hills ; I remember
a night at Dornholzhausen, where we slept in a barn.
In the early days of my stay the whole school was taken
to Frankfurt on the occasion of the fiftieth anniversary of
the Battle of Leipzig. I remember the sunny autumn
day, the immense crowds . . . then my waking up in a
strange room where several people were bending over
me. I had fainted in the crowd and been taken to the
nearest house.

My relations with Fräulein Hillebrand became steadily
worse in the course of years. According to her reports to
Mamma, I developed into a naughty and pugnacious girl.
One day an extraordinary thing happened to me. I was
standing in one of the class-rooms with several other
girls, having just come up from the dining-hall. Fräulein
Hillebrand passed and fixed her eyes upon me without
saying a word. I stood transfixed, spellbound. She
went out; I did not stir. The others went to their occupations ; I was left standing in the middle of the room. No
one spoke to me. Dusk fell, the lamps were lit; still I
was standing motionless, rooted to the spot. At last,
shortly before bedtime, one of the elder girls came up to
me with a message from Fräulein Hillebrand, saying that
I might go. An appalling experience, and one which
left a hurt in my soul from which it has never quite
recovered. But, thank God ! I had inherited a free and
independent spirit from my parents. I had had my
warning, and my tormentor never quite succeeded in her
subjection of me, although she left nothing untried.
Once she put her arm round my shoulders, drew me
towards her, and said, ' Cannot you have confidence in

me ? ' 'How can I have confidence in any one who has no confidence in me ? ' I quickly retorted. She pushed me away, saying, 'You are an altogether bad girl.' From that moment we were declared enemies, and she sent my poor mother the most alarming and, as I found out later, mendacious accounts of her youngest daughter.

I was longing perpetually for my mother and for Marie, and often cried myself to sleep. Days that brought letters from them were festivals, and I carried the letters about with me until they were in shreds. The fact that, contrary to my usual habit, I have carefully preserved every scrap of paper, shows how much value I attached to them.

EXTRACTS FROM MY MOTHER'S AND MY SISTER MARIE'S LETTERS FROM THE TIME WHEN I WAS IN RÖDELHEIM.

From Marie.

' DÜSSELDORF, 18 *October* 1863.

' MY DEAR EUGENIE !—We are going to Frankfurt next week, and shall come to see you as soon as possible. Mamma is well ; she was in Baden for only three days more, as she had to stay longer in Munich. It was hard to say good-bye to our dear cottage. Mamma and I cried when we left ; it was looking so dreary and desolate with closed shutters. . . .

' MARIE.'

From my Mother.

' WISMAR, 27 *November* 1863.

' You, my dear child, may not even know where to look on the map for the place whence I am writing to you. It is in Mecklenburg, where I am giving concerts : Schwerin, Rostock, Wismar, and Güstrow—look them out on the map, and while you are doing so think of your

Mamma who is always thinking of you, and especially now when you will soon be twelve years old, and advancing at every step towards being a young woman! I embrace you in the spirit, beloved Eugenie, on your birthday—to-morrow! I hope you will make good resolutions and renew them every day! I think my little presents will give you pleasure, and hope you will take care of the dressing-gown and not spoil it too quickly. Your last letter has pleased me very much, both in contents and style, but another time your handwriting must be better—a child should always find sufficient time to write carefully to its mother. . . . So farewell, my beloved Eugenie. A tender embrace from your devoted

'MOTHER KLARA.'

'DETMOLD, *December* 1863.

'DEAR GENCHEN,—You shall have a nice letter of Christmas greetings from me as well as your presents. May you spend the beautiful festive days happily, and afterwards write cheerfully to me about them, as you did the other day about your birthday. What a charming day that must have been! Dear, good Fräulein Hillebrand, how kind she has been to you! And how nice Christmas Eve will be, when not you alone but every one is celebrating the festal day! Think of me on that evening, dearest child. How I should love to see your enjoyment! How I shall think of you and your brothers and sisters! Julie will be the only one to be with me besides Marie. . . . I embrace you in truest love.—Your

'MOTHER KLARA.'

'Have you not yet made a special friend? If you have, give her my love.'

SCHOOL YEARS

From Marie.

' RIGA, 18 *February* 1864.

' MY DEAR LITTLE EUGENIE,—It is such a long time since you have heard from us, that you are probably quite cross with me. But I expect Elise and Julchen have written and told you what they know about us.

' We have now been in Russia for more than a week, or I should say in Livonia—for they speak German here, not Russian, and they have German ways and customs in all the families. The streets only look quite different from ours. When we arrived, there was deep snow as far as the eye could see ; all the people were driving about in open sledges, and for a few days, when there was a thaw, in open carriages. You hardly ever see a closed carriage, and it is difficult to understand why they are not used in this bitterly cold climate ; during the first days of our stay the wind was so frightfully cutting that we were always afraid of getting our faces frostbitten. The men wear big fur coats, and fur caps that cover their faces all but a little peephole for the nose. The poorer people wear sheepskins with the fur turned inside and the bare white leather outside ; their legs and feet are swathed in rags tied firmly with string, and they wear wooden soles on their feet. You may imagine what a strange impression all this made on me. I am now looking forward to St. Petersburg, although I like this place very much. We have been put up most kindly by a German family, and Mamma is worshipped by everybody. On Saturday we shall probably go to Mitau to give concerts. Mamma has played here at two : one on Sunday morning, the other last night. Unfortunately she is not quite well ; on our journey from Königsberg, which took twenty-four hours, she was very ill, and has not yet quite recovered. There is not a single town on the way from Königsberg where we could possibly have spent the night ; nothing but miserable villages or just groups of houses. The people are so frightfully poor that it wrings one's heart to see them. The hovels in which they live are tiny wooden sheds ; the little children standing in the doors are often barefoot, and with nothing but a chemise on them.

' You will have heard that we stopped in Berlin for a few days. We stayed with the Mendelssohns, and saw Ferdinand every day, who was well and cheerful. But poor Felix was in bed all the time. He has grown much taller since last summer, but he looks pale.

' We are longing to hear from you ; do be sure and write next Sunday, a long letter about everything : how you are, and what lessons you are doing—and what besides ? Has your little Christmas frock been made up, and how does it look ? Do you really like it ? It was my choice. I thought it would be becoming to you.—Your devoted sister, MARIE.'

' ST. PETERSBURG, 17-29 *March* 1864.

' MY DEAR EUGENIE,—We were very glad of your last news, as we could see from your letter that you were well and cheerful. We have now been in Petersburg for three weeks, and I like it very much—it is rather like Berlin, but much grander. The streets are very wide ; in the principal thoroughfares the houses are all palaces. The churches, too, are very fine, and have gilt cupolas that shimmer in the sun ; with the snow-covered roofs they make a beautiful picture. It had been snowing incessantly until the last day or two, when a thaw set in, and now the mud is so awful that walking is almost impossible. The streets are full of little sledges driven at a furious speed.

' We are staying at the Grand Duchess Helene's palace. She is a very cultured and artistic lady. Last Thursday

Mamma played at one of her soirées, when the Emperor and Empress were present.

'She has also played in public five times, and will probably give another concert. Next Friday or Sunday Mamma is to play at the Empress's palace.

'Last year at this time we were in Düsseldorf, do you remember? We went up to the Grafenburg with the Bendemanns on Easter Sunday and looked for Easter eggs.

'I am sorry to say that Mamma has not been at all well, and has not yet quite recovered.

'Farewell. An affectionate kiss from your devoted sister, MARIE.'

From Mamma.

'DRESDEN, 12 *April* 1865.

'DEAREST EUGENIE,—I thought that a pretty Sunday frock might give you pleasure, so I am sending you one which I fancied for my Eugenie. . . . Your sisters have the same, so for once you can all be dressed alike when you are home for the holidays.'

'BADEN-BADEN, 30 *September* 1865.

'I kiss you affectionately for your letters, especially for your dear birthday letter, which gave me real pleasure. We spent the day as cheerfully as we could. Your brothers and sisters gave me charming presents, Fräulein Leser sent me surprises, and at dinner-time Herr Levi arrived with champagne.

'The day before, the twelfth, was a trying one for me ; it was my silver-wedding day—what a happy day it might have been if your wonderful father were alive now ! I could not help thinking of it all day long, and it made me very sad. This was why, on my birthday too, I could not be really cheerful.

'Herr Joachim has been here for a fortnight with his

31

wife and charming little boy. In November we shall
give a concert together in Frankfurt; then I shall see
you, my beloved child. I cannot tell you how hard it is
for me to let Elise leave home—this separation makes me
dreadfully sad.'

' KARLSRUHE, 2 *May* 1866.

' MY PRECIOUS EUGENIE,—I have just received your dear
letter, which gave me so much pleasure that I must send
you a kiss in return at once. . . . It particularly pleases me
that you should wish to pass an examination, and makes
me happy altogether that you are industrious and eager to
learn. I am going through difficult days just now, as
Ludwig's obstinacy gives me great anxiety, so your letter
yesterday came like a ray of bright sunshine out of black
clouds. Continue like this, my darling child : it is
difficult to attain real merit in this world ; it means hard
striving against one's own weaknesses. But how wonderful it is when one has conquered them !—and with the
firm will you are showing I am sure you will succeed.

' I embrace you in warmest love, my dearest Eugenie ;
and when you find things difficult, think how happy you
are making your mother by your endeavours. That will
give you courage and perseverance.—Your devoted
' MOTHER KLARA.'

I had now been at Rödelheim for more than two years
and a half. I only saw my own people at rare and short
intervals during the whole of this time. In the first year
Fräulein Hillebrand gave permission for no more than a
week's stay at the Lichtenthal cottage ; in the second I
had four weeks' holiday. In between I never saw my
mother except when she came to Frankfurt, and that
meant a few hours only, there or at Rödelheim. My
sister Elise, who had settled as a piano teacher in Frankfurt in 1865, would have visited me every Sunday, but
Fräulein Hillebrand asked her to come only once every

MARIE, ELISE, LUDWIG, FERDINAND,
EUGENIE, AND FELIX

CHILDREN OF ROBERT AND CLARA SCHUMANN

four weeks. I corresponded regularly with my family, but, apart from the fact that children are bad correspondents, all our letters were censored by Fräulein Hillebrand, and this of course made unrestricted communication impossible. A certain amount of estrangement was the inevitable consequence, and it was not surprising that my mother should have had no suspicion of how unhappy I was.

This went on until June 1866. The summer was an excessively hot one ; the park was in its full beauty. Far removed from everything that happened in the outside world, we passed our days in work and play, in joys and sorrows. Then one day, to our boundless astonishment, we saw a number of strange men, perhaps sixty, march into the courtyard of the castle, soldiers in full equipment. They halted in the shade of the high plane-trees, threw off their packs, and lay down on the lawn. We soon learnt that they were Austrians, and that war was imminent. Our life was to go on as usual, except that we must confine ourselves to a restricted part of the park. Of course, we watched the strange inmates from the windows as much as we dared, and great was our surprise when we saw Fräulein Hillebrand ladle out soup from a huge cauldron suspended over an open fire.

A few days had passed, when we were told one evening at a late hour—it was quite dark—that another four hundred men had been quartered in the house, and that all the girls must leave.

The upheaval that followed this news may be easily imagined ; Fräulein Hillebrand must have had a few hours of terrible anxiety. Quarters had to be found for all the pupils, many of whom came from long distances. Each pupil whose home was close by, *e.g.* at Frankfurt, Höchst, Soden, Giessen, etc., had to take another girl with her. Conveyances had to be found, the most necessary things to be packed. How all this was accomplished I hardly know, but within a few hours we were

all on the road, and I found myself presently ringing the
bell in the middle of the night at my sister's house in
Frankfurt, or rather at that of the friends with whom she
happened to be spending a few weeks. I was received
most kindly by her hostess, and remained with them till
I continued my journey to Baden.

This was how it happened that I escaped from my
prison ; I was free, surrounded by my dear ones, and
saw all my brothers and sisters again. My relations with
my sister Julie became particularly close in the course of
this summer. I had always been in her confidence ; her
' petite confidente,' she used to call me, since French
came naturally to her after her long sojourn in France. I
was allowed to share in all her joys and sorrows. Otherwise I have no particularly vivid recollections of these
summer months. The days passed all too quickly, and
when I was suddenly told, ' Fräulein Hillebrand has
written to say you may return,' the news struck me like
a flash of lightning. I felt I could not possibly return
there, and I begged and prayed Mamma not to send me
back to Rödelheim.

At first she was angry, said she was sure of my being
well cared for at the school, and that I must return.
Then my despair broke all bounds ; I cried for a whole
day in Julie's room. For the first time I opened my
heart, and what I told Mamma must have shaken her
confidence in Fräulein Hillebrand, for the outcome was
that I never returned to Rödelheim. In the following
year an epidemic of typhoid broke out in the school, and
several pupils died. This may have been the reason why
Fräulein Hillebrand moved the school to Soden.

At the beginning of the Michaelmas term I was sent
to a smaller boarding-school at Neu-Watzum near
Wolfenbüttel. It was well spoken of, and was managed
by Fräulein Henriette Breymann, assisted by her sisters
Anna and Marie and her brother Karl. Once more I
came under the influence of an eminent woman, but how

34

great was the difference between those two ! I could not have told at the time in what the immense dissimilarity of their aims and outlook upon life consisted ; I could only feel it in its effect upon me. How different they were in outward appearance also ! Fräulein Hillebrand small, uncanny when she stealthily glided about ; Henriette tall and stately, dignified in her bearing and movements. Her features were not handsome, but her face was expressive ; her blue eyes might have been called luminous, if they had not been so very serious, almost melancholy. Struggles with the hardships of life and with delicate health had engraved themselves in the lines of her mouth. She was above all very human, and this was what attracted us most to her ; I did not realise this then as I have done since. She let us share in everything that concerned her and her family, and was on her side warmly interested in all the circumstances and experiences of her charges. She too had had to struggle with her own nature in the past, and this enabled her to understand others and all their ways, even when they went astray, and to use her influence with them to the noblest purpose. As she was the eldest of a large family, she had early learnt to help, advise, and support younger people. To us also she was a sister more than a superior, and the fact that we were asked to address her and her sisters with the familiar ' thou ' made us realise this. Her authority was unquestioned, yet we always approached her without fear. Our relations were founded on mutual confidence, and we felt that, though she demanded much of us, we should always find her a clement judge and a kind friend. Under the guidance of this safe hand I gradually recovered from the depression which had affected my whole being, and which had at first been my chief characteristic, as my fellow-pupils afterwards told me.

There was no question of a censorship ; full liberty in the exchange of letters with our families was taken as a matter of course. Once several mothers, including my own, had made complaints about our bad handwriting, and we were therefore told that the respective correspondents must show their letters to Henriette for a time. I can still see the half-veiled glance which she cast on the sheet while she quickly unfolded the letter and returned it to me, careful not to read a word.

The families of most of the pupils were in good circumstances, and the style of the school was in accordance with their requirements. Henriette, in consideration of the peculiar circumstances in our family, took me at reduced terms. But the Breymanns never let that make any difference ; I never felt at a disadvantage with the rich girls, as a sensitive child might easily have done. For love of my mother I always gave up of my own free will expensive amusements, such as excursions into the Harz Mountains.

Henriette often gave me concert tickets, and from time to time invited my brothers to stay, whom otherwise I rarely saw. In the course of the first term, however, a very distressing thing happened to me. Karl Breymann accused me of 'cribbing' from my neighbour during the arithmetic lesson. I was deeply hurt, indignant, and in the end, when he persisted in his accusation, desperate. Henriette, who had just returned from a long journey, and therefore had only known me a few days, called me to her room and said, ' If you can honestly tell me that you have not been cribbing, I shall believe you.' My answer must have been satisfactory, for she put her arm round me and said, ' I am sorry that you cannot convince Karl, but I believe you.' I was comforted, and at once became devoted to Henriette, heart and soul. The years which I spent under her tutorship belong to the happiest of my life. There have been difficult times ; I was combative by nature and not easy to deal with. I have caused Henriette much anxiety, but I succeeded in winning her affection. At a moment when I well-nigh despaired of myself, she comforted me with words never forgotten : ' You know, Eugenie,' she said, ' the girls who have caused one most anxiety are those to whom one often becomes most attached.' If I did not keep up the friendship with her afterwards as continuously as some of my fellow-pupils did, it was because I left school rather young, and henceforward lived my life among people whose aims and interests were not in touch with those of Henriette. But we have never been estranged, and I always felt certain of her kindness and benevolence towards me.

It is not for me to appraise Henriette's gifts and achievements. Others more fit for the task have done this, and what Henriette Breymann has done for women's education is sufficiently well known. She was an enthusiastic disciple of Pestalozzi and Fröbel, and devoted her whole life to pioneer work for the ideas of these great educationalists. Her aims went far beyond the limits of the Wolfenbüttel school, and when she married Karl Schrader, a member of the Prussian Diet, she was fully prepared for the great field of activity which awaited her in Berlin. Her two favourite pupils, Mary Lyschinska from Edinburgh and Annette Hamminck-Schepel from Holland, became my special friends, and I gave myself to friendship all the more exclusively and passionately because of the years of starvation at Rödelheim. Both these girls were my seniors by a few years, and had returned as students after they had finished their schooling, to be further initiated by Henriette into her own methods on Pestalozzi-Fröbel lines. Under her guidance they became leaders in education in the widest sense. Both devoted themselves entirely to their profession, and achieved much, one in England, the other in Germany. Mary Lyschinska held an appointment under the London County Council as Superintendent of Method in Infant Schools. Her special work was to introduce and explain Fröbel methods to Board School teachers at evening classes, and to inspect kindergarten and infant schools. She was the first woman to hold this post, as women had up to that time been disqualified.

Annette Schepel became part founder and head-mistress of the Pestalozzi-Fröbel House in Berlin until Frau Klara Richter took her place.

The relations of these two school friends of mine to Henriette were of a charming nature. They took care of her, nursed her through not infrequent illnesses, and relieved her of work whenever they could. Henriette's ideas took root in their hearts, and were disseminated by them in wider fields. One or the other was usually with her after her marriage. They filled the place of children of her own, which were denied to her, and it was therefore natural for Mary to remain with Herr Schrader after Henriette's death, to brighten his last years with filial love and devotion.[1]

I would like to mention two other fellow-pupils. Hedwig Krüsemann, who later married Kommerzienrat Heyl, was one ; she showed an early understanding of Henriette's aims, which, during a very active life, she made her own. The other was Charitas Dietrich, of the tragedy of whose young life I then had no knowledge. I understood it when I read her memoirs, incorporated in her biography of her mother, which she published under the title of *Amalie Dietrich, von Charitas Bischoff*.

I can only repeat that I was very happy in these surroundings. Neu-Watzum became a second home to me. My natural proclivity was to give myself up whole-heartedly to surroundings in which I lived, to people whose lives I shared—indeed, to the point of exclusiveness. My mother's fears that I might become estranged from her and my brothers and sisters were not unjustified. The thought of leaving the school grieved me deeply, and

---

[1] Since I wrote this chapter Messrs. Walter de Gruyter & Co. have published a work by Mary Lyschinska, collected and annotated by her, entitled *Henriette Schrader-Breymann : her life in her letters and diaries*.

long after I had said good-bye, the longing for all that I had left behind remained with me.

' DÜSSELDORF, 24 *December* 1866.

' . . . Your letter of the twelfth inst. gave me great pleasure ; it was of the kind which I enjoy receiving from one of you. But you have put yourself in the wrong with your friend Lamont. Think of what you yourself would have felt if you had asked her for her autograph and she had passed off some one else's on you. That was really insulting to her. Remember how often perfect strangers ask me for my autograph, how inconsiderate it is of them, how it bothers me and takes up my time, yet I should never have the heart to refuse. How much more would a friend feel a refusal ! Do you not feel how hard you have been upon her ? Believe me, my dear child, intellectual gifts are a great addition to life, but the real treasure, which lends brightness to it as nothing else does, is a kind heart. . . . Your little four-part exercise is very nice—go on, you will improve steadily.'

' LONDON, 25 *January* 1867.

' Our crossing to England was very disagreeable ; we were caught in a blizzard and wet through, as we remained on deck (but not sea-sick). As the Dover-London train left at once, we had to get in in our dripping clothes and sit in them for another two and a half hours. Fortunately we took no harm, except that a sty in Marie's eye, which had begun in Düsseldorf, grew to an enormous size and troubled her for a week. I have had a very exhausting time since I came, playing at concerts in quick succession in five different towns. Our reception has been most enthusiastic, and Herr Joachim and I and

Herr Piatti had to give encores everywhere. Travelling is made as comfortable as possible for us, well-heated compartments and rooms in the best hotels are always reserved, and the snow has fortunately never delayed us more than an hour or two. Trains go at an enormous speed—that is quite true ; but it frightens one less when one is in them than when one hears about it at a distance. But we have suffered terribly from the cold, for their open fires are warming only when one is standing close in front of them ; at one's back the wind blows in through chinks in doors and windows, and, to make matters worse, people are always leaving the doors open. We are staying here till Tuesday : on Tuesday I am playing in Bath, Wednesday in Clifton, Thursday in Torquay ; on Friday we return and stay here on the first, second, third, and fourth. On the first I am making my first appearance in London, on the fifth in Liverpool, sixth in Bradford ; on the seventh I return to London, where I am playing again on the ninth. I shall be thankful when all this is over, for it is an enormous exertion, as I have to travel for three or four hours on every concert day—from London to Liverpool even five and a half. Now you know our programme exactly, and all the places where we are going, and can accompany us with your thoughts day by day. . . .

'Now as to your affair concerning Herr Breymann. I cannot think that you are doing right, for even if Herr Breymann has wronged you the fact remains that he is your teacher, and one should never be in revolt against a teacher, never speak of him as you are doing. The feeling of gratitude should forbid that, for except one's parents there is no one to whom one owes so much gratitude as to a teacher who devotes his whole life to the good of other people's children. I believe that the time will come when you will see this for yourself, even though you are unable to do so at the moment, and when you will think of my words—may it be soon ! Moreover, it

MARIE SCHUMANN
IN HER TWENTY-SECOND YEAR

happens to people of all sorts and conditions occasionally to be under a false suspicion, often from those they love most dearly. If it is impossible to clear oneself, one must bear it, knowing that one is being *wronged*. But one should not revolt on that account : least of all against a teacher, for teachers have to do with many and difficult characters, and might easily make the mistake of suspecting an innocent person, because they are so often *really* deceived. Therefore do not take it so much to heart ; what matters most is that you should have nothing to reproach *yourself* with.

From Marie.

' RUGBY, 25 *April* 1867.

' There is a large Boys' Public School in Rugby, with five hundred boys in it. We are staying with the headmaster, Mr. Arnold, and we shall meet fifty of the pupils at dinner. That will be a quaint experience. This afternoon there is to be a football match in front of the house, which we are to watch. English people seem to think a great deal of these games ; last night the youth who is best at games was introduced to us, and specially commended on that account, as in our country the pupil who is best at his work would be specially mentioned. . . .'

From Mamma.

25 *April* 1867.

' . . . Your accounts of your life have interested me very much, and I am glad that you have found several friends of whom you are fond. I am also pleased to hear of your being sometimes asked to play to people ; that is quite good practice for you. . . . Your mistake in the Adagio from the Sonata Pastorale has made me laugh very much, for—fancy ! the same thing happened to me when I was first studying this sonata, but I—God knows why !—played the last six bars in the major. I think it must have been because the figure from the passage in the major in the middle of the Adagio returns quite at the end, that I dropped into the major. A thing like that is certainly annoying, as it is due to want of attention, but it should not make one furious. That would be unseemly in any man or woman, but especially in a woman, to whom gentleness only is becoming. Temper degrades when it gets the upper hand, and is altogether unworthy of us. Think of this always, my beloved child, when you feel your temper rising, and you will find that you can get the better of it. I have experienced it myself in former days, and now nothing grieves me more than when I occasionally lose my temper. Real religious feeling seems to me to consist chiefly in constant, constant work at ourselves, to make ourselves better and better, to live as much as possible for the good and the benefit of others, to be kind to every one with whom we come in contact. After all, it is the performance of these duties which gives the best kind of satisfaction ; of course, intellectual progress should go on as well. Our task is not easy, and we have to continue with it all through life ; it must be begun early, for it is much more difficult later on. . . . I am so glad that you are so fond of Fräulein Henriette ; I wish it could be so also with Herr Breymann. If it is on account of the affair which happened a little while ago, you must try to forget it—it is a pity to sulk, especially with a teacher, whose patience is often sorely tried. Now, my precious child, I must stop. Write again soon : the smallest thing you tell me interests me, and letters from my children are the only things which make the separation from them bearable to me.'

' BADEN-BADEN, 5 *August* 1867.

' . . . The rest of your letter has, however, pleased and interested me very much. I am always so glad when I hear of all that you are doing, so that I can keep up with it. Giving lessons is excellent practice,[1] not only intellectually, but helpful in teaching patience ; and nothing makes one appreciate what teachers have done for us, and the trouble they have taken, more than an attempt to give lessons oneself. Unfortunately, this knowledge often comes so late that we no longer have a chance of showing our gratitude to the teachers. But with you that is not yet the case, and I hope you will repay your teachers' trouble with willingness and kindness. Be sure to thank Fräulein Vorwerk for taking an interest in you musically. It is really very good of her. That reminds me of what you wrote about compliments which people paid you at Fräulein Vorwerk's matinée.[2] What Fräulein Henriette said to you can only have been meant as a joke, for if you answered people who meant to be pleasant to you in such a way, they would take it as an insult and say, ' What a preposterous, conceited manner the girl has ! ' When people pay a child compliments on her parents' account, nothing is required but that she should be glad of it ; a look of pleasure in her face is quite enough ; no clever repartees are expected from a young girl.

' How gladly I would have let Felix come to you ! . . . We were so pleased with him, he is such a charming

[1] The French mistress fell ill, and I was delighted when Henriette asked me to take over the French grammar lessons for a few weeks. I do not know whether my work satisfied her, but I distinctly remember one little episode. A pupil asked me in the course of the lesson whether it was ' le bonheur ' or ' la bonheur.' No doubt I really knew, but I became confused at the unexpected question and hesitated for a moment, when the expression, often used in Germany at that time, ' à la bonne heure ! ' crossed my mind, and I answered, ' la bonheur.'

[2] I had complained to Henriette that people were always saying the same things to me about my parents, and that I never knew what to answer. We were in the habit of talking quite frankly to her about everything, and she encouraged these confidences by her kind interest. She said on this occasion that Jenny Lind had often replied to compliments from her admirers, ' Yes, it is a heaven-sent gift.' Henriette had certainly not intended that I should give this answer ; my account to Mamma must have been misleading.

rascal ! . . . Sometimes he plays the violin really delightfully, but he has not enough technique. . . .'

'*Tuesday*, 15 *October* 1867.

(Written in pencil on a scrap of paper.)

' MY BELOVED EUGENIE !—You will be surprised to
receive these lines through a fellow-pupil. I met her in
the train at Giessen, and when she got in and I heard
them talking of Wolfenbüttel, I felt at once that I must
send my beloved Eugenie a line. You will be still more
surprised to hear that I am travelling by myself. Fancy !
Marie and Elise started this morning for Paris with
Josephine Schmitt and young Robert, to see the exhibition.
It took a great deal of persuasion before Marie would let
me travel alone, but at last I prevailed. As it is such
a splendid opportunity for them both, I was greatly
delighted to be able to give them this pleasure—a grand
sight like that is a remembrance for a lifetime, and I hope
they are enjoying themselves thoroughly.'

' HAMBURG, 24 *October* 1867.
' *Holzdamm No.* 8.

' . . . I am thinking so much of you and about you,
and you are right in thinking that you often make me
feel anxious, but that is all the more reason why my heart
will never weary of encouraging you again and again.
Your letter of yesterday, however depressed it sounded,
confirms me in my hope that you too will ultimately
make me happy, for I am convinced that you are doing
your best to become a thoroughly efficient girl. The
hardest thing for you is the struggle with your brusque
nature, but this struggle is our highest duty. When you
have succeeded for a time in controlling yourself, gentler
ways will grow upon you more and more, until they
become second nature to you ; you will gain people's
hearts, make your mother very happy, and your depression will disappear. You say you wish you were dead—

do you think so little of your sisters' lot in life ? Are they
not a prop to me, and the dearest friends of my heart ?
And are you not as dear to me as they ? Shall I not hope
to find you the same, my beloved child ? May *this
thought* make you as happy as it makes me ! Cherish it
in your heart before every other, and do not trouble
yourself about the future and what will become of you.
For the present *learn* all you can, then come home to me
and your sisters ; we will not let you want for work of some
kind in the house, and, please God, we shall yet live
together for a while. If you are anxious for outside
activity, that could be managed without our having to
part from each other. Above all, have courage and all
will be well. . . . I wish I could always be with you and
give you courage. When we see more of each other, I
am sure I shall be able to help you in your struggle against
the evil spirit which all of us more or less have to combat.'

' FRANKFURT, 1 *January* 1868.

'. . . Elise told me to-day what Fräulein Vorwerk
had said about interpretation. Do not take it to heart,
dear child ! Put your own feeling into the music which
you are playing. Even if it is not always the right one,
I would rather have that than none at all, or merely
what you have been taught. I think we shall understand
each other about this in the summer. . . .'

Fräulein Vorwerk, to whom this letter refers, was a
friend of Henriette's, living in Wolfenbüttel in comfortable
circumstances. She was most kind, and, being a devoted
admirer of my parents, offered to give me piano lessons.
She was a good pianist herself, and took no end of trouble
with me ; but her constant demands that I should tell her
what I had in my mind when I was playing a particular
piece of music, or what I thought the composer had had
in his mind, were exceedingly irksome to me. I usually
had nothing particularly in my mind, at least nothing that

45

I could have described in so many words. These cross-examinations were becoming quite a trouble to me, which I had confided to Elise. Curiously enough, I once caught myself in the same mistake many years later when I was a teacher myself; fortunately, the first attempt cured me for ever of it. A very talented pupil, twelve years old, had been studying the ' Papillons,' op. 2, by Schumann, and played them so charmingly that even Mamma was satisfied. Then it suddenly occurred to me to ask the girl what was in her mind when she was playing these pieces, and I told her to write a little sketch of what each suggested to her. When she brought me the paper, I was made aware that No. 5, which she played with great charm, had suggested to her : ' In this piece an elderly widow is dancing by herself, and wishing that her dear defunct were alive and dancing with her.'

I felt crushed, but I had learnt my lesson.

From Mamma.

' BRUSSELS, 14 *January* 1868.

' . . . We have been here for five days, and are staying till the twenty-third, when we leave for London. The day before yesterday I played Papa's Concerto at the Théâtre National to an audience of three thousand people, and was so enthusiastically received that I just longed for you all to be present. In Germany (North) the audiences have no idea of how to show their enthusiasm ; and though I do not think much of applause as a rule, there is no doubt that it stimulates an artist to see the audience so warmly appreciative.'

' LONDON, 16 *February* 1868.
'31 *St. James' Street, Piccadilly.*

' MY BELOVED EUGENIE,—I will answer your letter at once, and have already written to Fräulein Breymann. My dear child, you know that I like to give you pleasure

46

in every way I can, and think right. But it goes against my feeling that one's own pleasure should be considered first when one wants to help the poor. Think of it : if you all were to put together the money which will be spent in fancy dresses, it would amount to a good round sum, and you would still have the pleasure of the lottery whether in fancy dress or not. Besides, I cannot possibly afford expenses of this kind. You know I do not grudge you a real pleasure, but I should be most unwilling to spend money on a fancy dress which will only be worn once. If, however, all the others are doing it, I do not wish you to be an exception, but I should certainly not spend more than twelve shillings for this purpose.

' Marie wrote to you the other day. You did not mention it or thank her in your last letter. Write as soon as you can and tell us how you have managed ; but write to Marie—it will be for me as well. She easily feels hurt, and then I am so sorry for her, for she loves you all so dearly and thinks so much of you. Good-bye, my beloved child. An affectionate kiss from your devoted
' MOTHER KLARA.'

I see from Marie's letter of March 23, 1868, that I gave up the fancy dress. She writes : ' We are so glad that your bazaar brought in so much money, and that you enjoyed yourself just as well without fancy dress.'

The thought that Mamma had to earn every penny I needed with ' the work of her hands ' often troubled me when I was a mere child, and I hated to have to ask for new clothes.

' DÜSSELDORF, *April* 1868.

' MY BELOVED EUGENIE,—Although I cannot come to you on this auspicious day,[1] I shall be with you in the spirit, my beloved child, and take you in my arms, praying Heaven to grant all the desires of a mother's

[1] Confirmation.

47

heart. May the path of your life be a happy one, and may you brighten the lives of those with whom you come in contact, by faithful performance of your duties, kindliness, and modesty, and through this make me happy also —they are a woman's greatest charm, and will win her every heart. I will say no more than this, nor give you good advice. Wherever life leads you, may your heart show you the best way to turn !

' Let the enclosed brooch with your wonderful father's portrait be a remembrance of this day to you ! May our dear one be your pole-star ! he was a beautiful character in the highest sense of the word. Great in spirit, in heart, and in modesty, one to be looked up to in loving admiration. . . .'

' KARLSBAD, 19 *May* 1868.

' MY BELOVED EUGENIE,—You would have had a letter from me long before this, if I could have done all I wanted. But letters of importance which had to be answered without delay arrived daily, and I must not write much, because it always tires me. But now I will first kiss you for your dear letters—the last especially has been a heartfelt pleasure to me. I cherish the hope that you too will draw near to me in confidence as your sisters have done, who long ago learnt that there is no one in the world nearer and dearer than one's own parents. And thank God I can say that my heart is still young, so that I can understand young people, however youthful their feelings may be. I am looking forward with impatience to the time when I shall have you also to live with me : I think we shall come to know each other *intimately*— don't you think so, my own Eugenie ? . . . I hope to see Ferdinand during the Whitsun holidays, when I shall be in Berlin. I have thought a great deal about letting you come there too, and it worries me to have promised this to you ; since then I have had so many unexpected expenses that I cannot manage it.

' I hope for better times, and then my darling Eugenie shall not be stinted—in fact, none of you children, for you are all that I am living for.'

' ST. MORITZ, 6 *July* 1868.

'. . . First of all I will answer some of the things in your letter. I have written to Fräulein Breymann about your examination, and asked her for particulars. . . . The time advances with my advancing years when I shall be earning less, and I must now aim at giving you the best possible education, so that you may soon be independent. Unfortunately, Ludwig is no support to me ; on the contrary, I shall have to get accustomed to the thought that I may have to support him permanently. Felix is still very young, his education has only just begun. Poor Julie is so delicate that she cannot do anything for her livelihood, so there will be only Ferdinand and you on whom I can count (besides Elise, who has been independent for years). I am going so carefully into all this, because I want you to realise how important your career is for you. I am confident of your becoming an efficient, conscientious woman like Elise, and making me happy. That will be so, my beloved Eugenie, will it not ? I shall not be disappointed. You have abilities ; and if you have not the creative musical gift, do not make yourself unhappy on that account, and think that you have no imagination. I am sure you have imagination—perhaps not as much musically as is necessary for a *productive* artist, but enough for a *reproductive* one, and that will quite satisfy me. I myself should be unable to produce the smallest poem. I believe that what is understood by imagination is not only inventive faculty, but also understanding of the imaginative.

' Mary Lyschinska is indeed quite right to tell you not to throw away your imagination on *trifles*, such as meeting trouble half way, getting yourself into a state of excitement, and so forth. One should never get into a state of excitement about nothing, and on no account whatsoever waste feelings on trifles. There are quite enough great sorrows to be borne. Enjoy your life while it is free from cares. As long as I am alive, I hope I may be able to keep them from you, and my best way now is to do what I can for your education as well as for your health.

' What you tell me about the Beethoven Sonata in F sharp major has not surprised me at all. It is impossible for you to be attracted by it, for it is one of the things that demand considerable maturity on the part of the executant, and this cannot be expected of you—you are still too young. Even if you were an *artist*, you would be too young to understand it.

' I cannot tell you what is likely to happen about you in the future. . . . Do not worry about that, my dear ! Think only of your education for the present, not only so far as your intellectual training is concerned, but also that of your character, for that matters most. I could not live with any one whose heart and intellect are not in harmony ; and if I had to do without one of the two, I would rather do without intellect than without heart.

' Now some of our news. We arrived three days ago, and here we are, at an altitude of 6000 feet above sea-level, surrounded by snow-clad mountains and little woods ; in the foreground a beautiful green lake. But it is cold ! We had a blizzard all day long on the first day, and only to-day the clouds have lifted a little and allowed us a glimpse of the outlines of the enormous rocky peaks. The air is wonderful, we are feeling the effect already ; and the iron and oxygen waters are most enjoyable. I take baths, Elise drinks the waters.

' But the drive up here was positively terrifying. Imagine that we had to drive for hours along the brink of an abyss ; rocks sky-high on one side, a precipice on the other ; and the road so narrow that when two carriages meet, one must draw quite near the edge (where down below a torrent wildly rushes over rocks), or even stop. Never shall I forget the terror I endured, stuck inside that diligence. But it is nature at its grandest and most wonderful, almost overwhelming in its wild austerity. I hope I may be able to take you also to see scenery such as this. But grandeur in nature, just as grandness in art, demands a certain maturity, and only experience, and even trials, will make us really appreciate it.

' *P.S.*—If you are going to produce a new handwriting next time, do not forget to put your name, else I do not know who it is ! If I were you I should improve the old handwriting instead of trying quite a new one. But—do as you like about it ; it is not very important.'

From Marie.

' BADEN, 15 *September* 1868.

' . . . Will you let me have a complete list of your winter clothes and tell me what you need ? There are some good dresses of Mamma's which we will send you if you need them, and you can have them altered. '

By way of a commentary to this letter :—

The dresses were sent, including a brocade, a sea of silver flowers on a black ground—wonderful, indestructible, but not exactly suitable for a girl of sixteen, and this girl was perfectly miserable about her new Sunday frock. I dressed with a heavy heart and left my room reluctantly, to meet my fellow-pupils, when I saw Henriette coming towards me. Her eyes grew large as she looked at me, and she said, with the little mischievous twinkle which sometimes lurked in their corners, ' Oh, but what a charming dress you are wearing, Eugenie ! '

Of course, I felt cheered. What perfect tact, what understanding of young people, were underlying these few words !

MEMOIRS OF EUGENIE SCHUMANN

From Mamma.

' FRANKFURT A/M., 11 *October* 1868.

' MY BELOVED EUGENIE,—I cannot tell you how sorry I have been for the unfortunate mishap by which you and Felix missed each other, and he got into the wrong train at Guntershausen !

' But I will make you a splendid reparation, even though I have to put my hand in my pocket ; my soft heart insists that you should still have the pleasure of meeting each other. Well, then, my dear Eugenie, I shall return from Bremen on November the fourth, and you will be waiting for us on the platform in Wolfenbüttel with your bag and little suitcase, and come to Berlin with us. We shall stay there together for four days—on the ninth we depart for Breslau, and you will return. What do you think of this plan ? Will my dear Eugenie give me a really good kiss for it ? . . .

' Give Fräulein Breymann my best thanks ! I hope she will not mind the little excursion to Berlin ! . . . I am very busy, so cannot write more, but the great pleasure will make up for a short letter ! A tender embrace from your   KLARA.

' We shall be staying at an hotel in Berlin : we will live like gods—I mean, as happily. We could not be quite unrestricted if we were staying with friends, whom one must consider, so I will not ask any one to take you in, but have you with us. But mind you bring a nice dress with you as well as a decent one for everyday ; the flannel one will do for that, and the black silk for going out. Once more, addio ! '

' VIENNA, 29 *November* 1868.
' *Stadt Operngasse* 6.

' . . . I can give you good news of myself : again I have been received with open arms ; the audience welcomed me at my first concert a week ago as though they really

loved me. That was a great joy to me ! Two crowded
concerts are now over ; I shall give a third on December
the fifth, and probably a fourth on December the four-
teenth. They have been trying again on every side to
persuade me to settle here. I should not hesitate for a
moment if Vienna were not so far from the centre of
Germany ! . . . Herr Brahms is here, and played Papa's
Variations for two pianos with me at yesterday's concert.
He is very nice and charming to us, and we owe him many
pleasant hours. We are most comfortable at the Osers' ;
when it is so exceedingly difficult to get rooms, one
appreciates hospitality the more. People are all so good
to us ; life in Vienna is still cosy and simple, not as in other
capitals, although the town has grown enormously.

' I am having good news from Lix and Ferdinand.
Lix writes charming letters in his own thoughtful and
often poetic way. Write again soon ; letters from you
children are the best thing that happens to me. . . .'

Marie adds :

' We see a great deal of Brahms, who is staying here.
Mamma played the Variations for two pianos with him
yesterday, *i.e.* in the original version, with accompaniment
of two 'cellos and a horn.'

From Marie.

' LONDON, 24 *January* 1869.

' . . . We have been here since the night before last.
Had a splendid crossing : such a beautiful dark-blue sea
with little white crests ; it looked lovely. There is no
doubt, England is a charming country ; everything looks
green and luscious even in winter : only London is choked
with coal smoke—an atmosphere to which it is hard to
get used. The sky is always grey.

' We were met at the station by a friend, Mr. Burnand ;
he took us to his beautiful house, where we shall stay until

we have found rooms. He and his sister received us with a kindness which made us quite forget that we are in a foreign country. We are surrounded by love and care and every imaginable comfort. It is a pity that we cannot stay on here : we shall feel the difference when we go into lodgings. . . . To-morrow we are going to Manchester for the concert on Tuesday ; to Liverpool on Wednesday, Preston on Thursday ; on Friday we return to London, where Mamma will play for the first time this season on Saturday at noon, and where we shall stay during the week after next, Mamma playing on Monday, Wednesday, and Saturday.

' It is nice to think that you are looking forward to the summer ; you will see how cosy it can be at home, although we cannot give you all the school interests and pleasures.   MARIE.'

From Mamma.

' BRUSSELS, 13 *April* 1869.

' DEAREST EUGENIE,—I will send you a word myself at last, and kiss you for your dear letter. As you see, we have left England, and shall be going to Düsseldorf to-morrow to stay for a few days. Be prepared to start at a moment's notice ; from Düsseldorf I will let you know when we shall expect you, probably in Frankfurt. Marie will take you with her to Baden to get the cottage ready ; she will be glad of your help. I shall arrive a little later. . . .

' Good-bye, my beloved Eugenie ! How I am looking forward to having you with me altogether at last ! . . . One more word : be sure to ask Fräulein Breymann what she advises you to study during the summer—it is so important that you should make progress, not go back. . . .'

These are a few extracts only from a considerable number of letters which my mother wrote to me between my fifteenth and eighteenth years. As I said before, I

ELISE SCHUMANN
IN HER TWENTIETH YEAR

cherished them as my most precious possession at the time, but I have realised their full value only now when I am well advanced in years. Mothers have loved, felt, written like this since the creation of the world. But that a woman who had dedicated herself to art, an art sufficient in itself to fill a whole life, and whose performances demanded a constant high tension, could also in the highest and widest sense of the word be a mother, seems to me nothing short of a miracle : I should say unique.

I was merely one of the seven children, and Marie the only one living with my mother ; the other six were scattered about the world. They had not only to be provided for, but to be written to. Yet these letters, mostly written on concert tours, in rare moments snatched from travelling, rehearsals, concerts, visitors, and other interruptions, show no trace of superficiality or hurry. Attention was given to all that I had written, not the. slightest detail was forgotten ; they speak of love that never wearied, of anxiety which often gave her sleepless nights. Dear Mother ! How she strove to win my confidence, how she dreaded estrangement after so many years of separation ! And now these were over ; I was grown-up, and took my place with the others in the home which this affectionate mother had created for us, truly with ' the work of her hands.'

BROTHERS AND SISTERS

HEAVEN had bestowed its gifts in beautiful symmetry on my parents: three girls, three boys, a girl, a boy. I never knew the eldest boy, Emil, who died in 1847. But you others—let me call you forth, beloved ones who are still on this earth, and you who have long left your mortal frame behind ! Pass before my soul once more ; let me see you as you were when we all met during that memorable summer ; let me survey the course of your lives, and describe each strongly marked and lovable personality.

Marie, Elise, Julie ! Your first steps in life were guided by our father, and it was for you that he started to write the 'Little Book of Memories' to which I have already referred, and which he continued for three years. What love, what understanding, while he watched the first efforts of your little feet, the first manifestations of your souls ! How much did you, did we all, lose in this father !

MARIE

In the following letter to our grandmother in Berlin he tells of her—his firstborn's—entrance into this world :—

'*Wednesday*, 1 *September* 1841.

'DEAR MAMMA,—You are the grandmamma of a charming, well-fashioned little girl. There is great rejoicing in our house. But there were also three anxious hours of great suffering for Klara. She is now quite well, quite happy. Court-Physician Jörg, who assisted when Klara was born, has now also assisted with Klara's child. If you could only be with us ! You would see

56

happy human beings. Auntie has been a faithful help ; she came at four o'clock in the morning. Certain symptoms became apparent last night, labour began towards six in the morning, and at twenty minutes past ten the little creature was born. Her first cry—and we fell into each other's arms, weeping. Klara herself was as though she had been reborn. Good-bye, dear, kind mother of my Klara, grandmother of—what shall we call her ? Write at once to your

' HAPPY CHILDREN.'

> ' " Gay as a lark " is my device,
>   And on this happy day,
>   Dearest Mamma, take my advice
>   And be for ever gay.'
>
> MARIE.

Little four-year-old Marie presented these words, ' written by Papa for September 13, 1845,' to her mother on her twenty-sixth birthday. This ' gay as a lark ' developed early into sympathetic, even-tempered cheerfulness which even the tragic event that clouded the early years of her girlhood could not long banish from her disposition. Memories of both parents, with whom she had spent her happy childhood, were a charm which ever after shed a gentle brightness upon the laborious path of her long life. She was the only one of us who retained a distinct impression of our father's personality, cherished it in her heart, and shared it with us.

When I wrote the memories of my childhood, it was you, Marie, who stood out prominently. You were a second mother to me, a refuge. I clearly remember that the little child, that was I, loved your face, your eyes of deep blue-grey with thick eyebrows, your smooth, lustrous black hair, your slender figure. I know that I liked to cuddle up to you and breathe the faint, warm perfume of your hair. Your health was magnificent, and you were always cheerful, always contented. After difficult times you would recover your balance surprisingly quickly, and thereby become a support to the weaker ones. You had a great sense of humour, and when you laughed the tears ran down your cheeks. You were a tease, and Mamma used to say you had inherited that from Papa. But in spite of your equanimity you had a distinct tendency to ' furor teutonicus,' which would break like a thunderstorm and as suddenly pass. You were also the thoughtful one in the family. Goethe was your favourite author even when you were quite young ; he moulded and guided your mind. You often brooded long and tenaciously in silence over some important or unimportant matter, and we always knew that what Marie had been thinking over would come to a good end.

Your existence was inseparably bound up with our mother's. You had been our father's favourite, and this was a great tie between you. You had been young together, and you have told me that you can remember the time when she used to sing softly to herself. You two knew no life apart from each other. Once we had all persuaded you to accept an invitation to Paris. All your arrangements had been made, your boxes packed. I was looking forward to carving in your absence and taking over other duties. At the last moment you declared you would not go ; all our entreaties were in vain. We had to send telegrams to say you were not coming ; you unpacked your boxes, and I never learnt to carve.

You were never really happy unless you took care of our mother and us from morning till night, and of many others as well. Your thoughts were exclusively occupied with our wellbeing ; no other life appealed to you. Even now, aged and bereft of many whom you took under your wings, you are still filling up the gaps from the younger generations who have never seen you face to face.

BROTHERS AND SISTERS

You, more than any of us, were the guardian of memories of our parents. You set your steps in the path marked out by their spirit; and though you have never said so, I know you have striven unremittingly to be like them. You will reach your goal!

I had to fulfil my own destiny, which parted my life from yours; but wherever it led me, when my feet carried me back to you, then—and only then—did I know that I had come ' home.'

ELISE

You were the most original of the whole crowd. Tall and slim you were, strongly built, with blue eyes and thick plaits of fair hair round your head. Striking features, not unlike our mother's, and quick, impulsive movements showed your determined spirit. Very early you began to build up your life with a firm hand; your desire for independence and for sharing our mother's burdens showed you your way. You left the shelter of the maternal roof to live amongst strangers; you went to Frankfurt a/Main, where you settled as a piano teacher. You were an excellent pianist as early as 1865. I remember a day when Mamma was playing Brahms' Quartet in A flat major from manuscript with the Florentine Quartet. She was called away, and the artists asked you to take her place. You sat down at the piano without the least embarrassment and played the difficult work as though you had always known it.

You never again became a permanent inmate of our house, but you remained devoted to us in sisterly affection. You shared our mother's cares and anxieties, helped where you could, and took the greatest interest in the development of the younger ones.

When you came to us for short holidays, it was as though a whirlwind had been raised in the house; your self-confidence, the lordly way in which you used to deal

59

with matters great and small, gave us no end of amusement. You had no hesitation in attempting things you had never done before, and would never be baulked. I remember a skirt which you offered to tailor for Marie, who had not had the courage to cut out the scanty material. Your quick hands readily seized the large scissors and set to work ; the skirt was prepared in no time, and looked very professional as it lay ready tacked ; but alas ! slender though she was, Marie could not get into it !

Whatever you were doing, you did it with all the passion underlying your nature. Not a word could we get out of you for hours when you were bent upon some occupation. A rhyming friend of ours singled out this peculiarity on the occasion of the merry evening preceding your wedding, when he said :

> ' You and General von Moltke alike
> In terrible silence brood—then strike.'

You were an altogether original creature. In the autumn of the year when you had settled in Frankfurt, Mamma and Joachim gave a concert there. Mamma thought this a good opportunity of introducing you to the Frankfurt public. She proposed to play our father's Variations for two pianos with you. You were exceedingly unwilling to play in public at all, but were finally persuaded. The day of the concert came ; I had come over from Rödelheim and was among the audience, heard the Kreutzer Sonata for the first time, and saw you appearing on the platform with our mother ; Joachim turned over for you. All went as well as possible ; the audience was enthusiastic. When it was over, Joachim said to you in the artists' room, ' Well, Fräulein Elise, don't you feel now how delightful it was to play with your mother in public ? '—and he got the unexpected answer, ' Never again ! ' Another time she asked him, ' I suppose that bit is very difficult ? ' ' What

makes you think so?' Joachim asked in surprise.
'Because you are always playing it out of tune.' 'Do
I really?' he said in the most charming manner. 'I
shall have to be careful about that.'

You always made straight for anything you wanted,
and never refused what the moment had to offer. When
happiness came your way, you would take firm hold of
it. You gained a good man's affection, who became a
true son to our mother, a kind brother to us. You have
had your share of sorrows ; but in looking at your life as
a whole, I can say that you have been one of fortune's
favourites. On September 13, 1845, when you were two
years and six months old, you presented to our mother
on her birthday these auspicious, truly prophetic words,
written by our father :—

> ' Geniesse
> Ist meine Devise.
> > Elise.'
> (Enjoy ! is my motto. Elise.)

JULIE

I must retrace my steps by fifty years to reach her !
Then, when the beloved form in its irresistible charm
comes back to me, I seek in vain for words to describe
her. I could speak of her eyes, blue as the sky, beautifully set in her face, and with lids that showed the delicate
veining. I could say that her hair, luminous as gold and
fine as silk, framed her exquisitely white forehead ; that
the lines of her nose were finely chiselled and her mouth
not too small, with sensitive lines in its curves ; that all
these features combined to form a face of such unusual
charm that no one could look upon it without joy. Yet
this would not convey the nobility which those features
expressed, their radiance, the sweetness of disposition, the
vivacity of her emotions and her mind.

She was a favourite of the gods, a girl of whom Brahms

once wrote to our mother that ' it is difficult to think of
her without emotion,' and alas ! beloved by the gods
also in that she died young.   Was the touch of melancholy,
the slight shadow which now and then darkened—no,
only veiled—for moments the radiance of her being, was
that a premonition of her fate ?   Or was it the shadow
of the past, the loss of her father ?   Or else the long
periods of separation from the mother she adored, from
brothers and sisters to whom she was devoted ?   Her life
among strangers, her delicate health ?   Probably all these
causes combined to give depth, firmness, dignity to her
character, gentle grace to her bearing, thus adding a
touch of greatness to her natural loveliness.

Life in the great world had helped to develop her
intellectual gifts, which were considerable and had been
carefully trained.   She learnt with ease, but constant
striving after perfection, an inheritance from our parents,
preserved her from superficiality.   Whatever she did,
down to the smallest domestic duty, she did with all her
heart and soul.   Gladly and easily she fitted herself into
our simple life during the summer, while she spent the
winter sharing in all the advantages which her life with
her wealthy hosts gave her, and thoroughly enjoying
them.   She was deeply, even passionately, attached to
the friends to whom she was entrusted for the winter
months, but the depth of her devotion was given to her
own family.

In the year 1868 she met the man who won her heart.
In the following year he took her to her new home in a
foreign country, where two motherless girls were waiting
for her affection.   She bore him two sons, fair and
charming ; all the sunny loveliness of her nature was
lavished upon him, his children, his home.   Three years
of radiant happiness were granted to them ; she was
bearing a third child—' Chiarina ' she called it in glad
anticipation.   But her strength was insufficient for the
new life.   She was called away to the land whence there

JULIE MARMORITO SCHUMANN
IN HER TWENTY-THIRD YEAR

is no return, leaving an immeasurable void which only time, patient time, has gradually filled with the warmth of sweet memories.

LUDWIG,

the eldest boy, was in his twenty-second year in the summer of 1869. Unlike his younger brothers, who were tall and slender, his was a broad and sturdy frame. He resembled our mother : his features were noble and expressive, and he had also inherited her complexion, low in tone, yet not colourless. A mass of black hair hid in a thatch the upper part of his fine forehead ; his magnificent dark-brown eyes had, as my mother used to say, an expression of indescribable sweetness and faithfulness, but there was also deep pathos, such as I have never seen in any other human being. In this summer we met for the first time after many years of separation ; I looked at him with the eyes of a grown woman, and my heart stood still. Young as I was, I realised what that look might mean. A premonition of the tragic fate which was to overtake him passed through my mind. His physique was powerfully developed ; his affections were warm and deep. He was devoted to us sisters and brothers, but above all to our mother. The sole aim of his life was to be a support to her, and he worked like a slave for this. But his mind had not kept pace with his body, and his development had stopped when he was still a child. His younger brother soon outstripped him at school. When I now look at the letters which he wrote as a boy, I cannot understand how we could ever have deceived ourselves about him, how we could have made him responsible for actions and peculiarities solely due to the state of his mind.

With the best intentions, he usually did the wrong thing. His self-absorption prevented him from measuring himself against others, and he was quite unable to judge his capacities. He proved it by deciding to take up a musical career after years of hesitation ; but though he was fond of music, he was entirely lacking in gifts. A most striking feature was his clumsiness, for which he was constantly blamed. As soon as he arrived at the house, some accident or other would happen : he knocked against something or somebody, or dropped a dish which he was passing. When these things occurred it was heart-breaking to see the pathetic look that came into his eyes.

When we were amongst ourselves Ludwig was charming, even demonstratively affectionate, and could be quite gay too. When his features became animated and his sensitive lips were parted in laughter, it was as if a ray of sunshine had dispelled the habitual gloom on his face, which then became very attractive.

He loved nature, and there was nothing that he enjoyed more than walks in the woods with us. Once he ran away ; all our calling and searching was in vain, we had to let him go his own way, and he did not return till many hours later. And on many occasions a strange, evil spirit came over him when he had been in quite a cheerful mood ; it seemed to seize him and make him blind and deaf to every warning, to all our love and entreaties. Those were only the beginnings. Who can tell what you, our beloved brother, have suffered in all the years that followed upon this summer, the last of your sojourns with us, years when you were separated from those you loved ; when your beautiful eyes lost their sight, and you mourned under restraint until death released you !

I have Ludwig's last letter before me, written from the asylum at Colditz in 1875, on the occasion of my twenty-fourth birthday, when he wrote : ' It was an extraordinarily great pleasure to see you again, however short our meeting, after long and painful years of separation. I am so short-sighted that I should hardly have recognised you, my dear and charming sister, but your

LUDWIG SCHUMANN
IN HIS NINETEENTH YEAR

memory is firmly imprinted on my mind, and nothing will take it from me. . . . I hope all our dear ones will keep their health, especially our beloved mother, for whose love and kindness we cannot be thankful enough to God ; her life is a precious and inestimable possession, and must be carefully watched over.'

Ludwig lived for another twenty-five years after this letter was written, but I never saw him again. The shadows closed more and more around him, and at last he became, as my mother often said in deep distress, ' buried alive.'

FERDINAND

The ' Little Book of Memories ' unfortunately comes to an end on July 5, 1849, and contains nothing about Ferdinand except the date of his birth, July 16 of that year. With his dark-blue eyes, abundant black hair, and very fair skin he too must have been a charming baby. While my father was still alive, Ludwig and Ferdinand were sent to school ; the latter must have been quite a little fellow at the time. We took it as a matter of course that we all had to leave home to grow up among strangers ; we felt it to be inevitable. When we suffered, it was with a sense of resignation ; we knew things were not the same with us as with other people. But when I now look back upon my brothers' lives, the tragedy of their fate fills me with indescribable sorrow. Their sweetness of disposition and purity of heart were unusually great ; they were attached to their mother and brothers and sisters with their whole soul ; intimate hours spent in the family circle had infinitely greater charm for them than outside attractions.

Yet this was the one thing which our mother could not give them. We girls also missed it, but the close companionship of our mother later in our lives made up for it. Our brothers, on the other hand, never knew what it was to have a real home.

Strangers guided their steps, and with the best intentions they cannot take the place of parents. Ludwig had not the gift of letting himself go ; he would press our hands until it hurt, and when, perhaps with a cry of pain, we looked at him, we saw his eyes craving for love, and we understood all that was passing in him, his longing for what he had never possessed.

Ferdinand was of a different, a more communicative disposition. In his letters he often complains of the separation from his mother and from us. This demonstrative affection gave him early a feeling of responsibility towards us, and this saved him from self-pity. The wish to be a support to our mother, to help her to bear her heavy burdens, was the aim and object of his life during his adolescence. When he had made up for what he had lost by changing schools three times, his progress was rapid, and he became one of the best pupils at the Joachimsthaler College in Berlin. In the year 1863 he wrote to me, who was then a girl of eleven :—

' . . . I am all right and getting on splendidly at school, and I am very glad about it. I am almost always top of my form. I had another prize on the anniversary of the Battle of Leipzig, October 18 ; that is my third. . . . I will write again for your birthday. Good-bye, dear Eugenerle ; think often of your awfully, 100,000,000,000 times devoted   BROTHER FERDINAND.'

And in the year 1865 : ' . . . I do a lot of carpentering. I want to make myself a workbox, but I don't know who is to give me the wood. Auntie has promised me all the sewing things I shall want for it. . . . I am giving Felix piano lessons ; he plays little selected pieces, but he does not get on very much—he can't, because he has no time to practise. . . . I shall probably get a remove to Ober-Secunda at Easter, go on at school until Michaelmas, and then—well, then I shall go into business, and I like the idea very, very much.'

66

Although Ferdinand was only two years my senior, he took a great interest in my education, and was not sparing of good advice and admonitions in his letters. In 1866 he wrote : ' . . . I was really rather cross with you for not having written, for when brothers and sisters have been together it is only good manners for the younger to write to the elder, and I never omit to do this myself. You might have done so all the more as you know how little time I have to give to anything except business. I hope you will soon answer this letter and tell me how you are, and other things that might be of interest to me. There have been many changes in my life since last we met. . . .'

Ferdinand had entered Herr H. C. Plaut's bank in Berlin, and had before him four years of apprenticeship, with hard work and no holidays except a few on special occasions. During this time he became an experienced man of business, and gained the respect and affection of his chief by his industry, conscientiousness, and absolute reliability. He wrote in 1867 : ' . . . As a rule I am cheerful ; I like my work very much indeed, and I have lately been transferred to another department where there is more variety, and where I read every order that comes in directly after Herr Plaut, which is interesting. . . . Julchen is back in Baden. I hope the poor dear girl is much better. How I wish I could see her again ! Felix is in Berlin too, and so jolly that it does one good to spend the Sundays with him.'

' *November* 1867.

' DEAR EUGENCHEN !—I am so glad you have put me under an obligation to write to you for your birthday. Even if it had not been my turn I should still have sent you good wishes, for I am not given to sulking ; but now that you have answered my letter, I write with all the greater pleasure. First of all, let me give you my heartfelt wishes. As you will spend your birthday with Mamma,

I need not wish you any other enjoyment, only good health, and that you may grow in wisdom and understanding and be industrious, so as to please Mamma. These are my wishes for you, but for myself I could wish you to think a little more of me and show it by writing more often than you do ; I am in hopes that you will. . . . I am enormously hard-worked in the bank ; but as this is what I like, it is probably good for me. In the evening, when I think over all the things which I have done in the course of the day, I feel really happy. I should so much enjoy seeing you again ; could it not be arranged for you to spend your holidays here? '

' *February* 1868.

' MY DEAR EUGENIE !—I have received your dear letter of January 12, and cannot repeat too often how very glad I am that you are thinking of us more than you did, and show it by writing to us. I can only say that the change is to your own advantage, for it makes us twice as fond of you. Our dear Julchen has probably arrived in Frankfurt by now ; she was due last Saturday. How glad I am that she has got on so far ! But it makes me sad not to have seen her, when I love her more than I can say. . . . You will have heard that Mamma is in London ; she is frightfully hard-worked, and that is why we are keeping everything from her that would distress and worry her, although there is cause enough.[1] . . . Felix's perseverance, good sense, and his affection for me make me daily fonder of him ; it is such a comfort to have him here. . . .'

' *April* 1868, *at night.*

' MY DEAR EUGENIE !—I had promised to write to you for your confirmation, and therefore regret all the more that this letter will be a day late. . . . To-morrow is the most auspicious day of your life, and we cannot have

---

[1] Refers to Ludwig's breakdown.

68

FERDINAND SCHUMANN
IN HIS NINETEENTH YEAR

too many good wishes for you. First and foremost, I trust that you will really understand the importance of this day and resolve to do right always, not only in faithfulness to your vow, but also to Mamma. Every day makes her invaluable goodness to us clearer to me, and you should do your utmost to give her satisfaction, and to us also who are so fond of you. I shall keep you and the solemn ritual in my mind to-morrow. To tell you the truth, I am very fond of you. You may not think so, but it is true all the same. I have sometimes been rather hard upon you, and you did not fail to pay me back in my own coin ; but then we were too young to understand what a precious possession brothers and sisters are to each other, and that their affection surpasses that which they feel for others. You too will have realised this by now, and I will pray to God to-morrow that He may draw us more and more closely together and bless our love. . . . I am sorry that I have nothing to offer you except these good wishes. I have already told you that I cannot give you a present for your confirmation ; you will not mind, will you ? I give you my love, as great as it can be ; will you give me yours in return for this frank confession of mine ? Write soon and tell me you are not going to disappoint me. . . .

' I am well, but I feel lonely and forsaken. Dear Lix,[1] who now often writes to me, was such a joy to me, and I am longing for the autumn, when, if it is God's will, I shall see him again. The only thing which makes up for his absence is that on Sunday afternoons, which I used to spend with him, I am now at liberty to do all sorts of things—study, read, do music, etc. I often go to Grandmamma's for dinner and stay the evening ; it is not particularly amusing, but I like to go because we have plenty to talk about, and I feel I am among my own people. Grandmamma is wonderfully young for her

---

[1] Felix had to stay away from school for six months on account of his health ; he stayed with our mother first in Karlsbad, then in Baden.

age ; she will be seventy-eight on May 15. How would
it be if you sent her your good wishes ? She would be
pleased, and would be sure to send you an answer. To
tell you the truth, she has none too good an opinion of
you, and your writing to her would prove that you
deserve better.'

' *March* 1869.

' I expect you have made enormous progress in music.
My attempts in this line are, as you may imagine, extremely modest. But music is so precious an inheritance
to me that nothing else gives me equal pleasure, and when
I sit down to play I give myself up to it with all my heart.
It is also very nice to have the chance of going to concerts
occasionally. . . . We are enormously busy at the bank
just now ; that means work at high pressure. In the
evenings I feel quite done up, after I have written letters
from 1.30 or 2 P.M. till 7 or 7.30 without a moment's
pause. Then when I get home, have made myself a cup
of tea, and sit down to play some sweet things by Papa,
Mendelssohn, or Beethoven, I feel refreshed, and even
equal to writing a love-letter of this kind. . . .'

In the summer of 1869 I only saw Ferdinand for a few
days when he came to Baden for Julie's wedding. But
during the following winter, which I spent in Berlin, I
became intimately acquainted with both him and Felix ;
and the more I have thought about them since I began
to write these Memoirs and read their letters, the more
I have become convinced that no mother could have
wished for better sons. A tragic fate overtook them :
both succumbed to incurable disease, Felix quite young,
Ferdinand as a middle-aged man. This cast a load of
sorrows and anxieties on my mother's heart, but how
could my poor brothers be blamed ? Whenever my
mother spoke of Ferdinand, it was with affectionate
pride. She said that he had never given her a moment's

anxiety until the first symptoms of his disease showed themselves after the war of 1870-71.[1]

Her faithful friend and adviser, Franz Mendelssohn, head of the great banking firm, wrote to her in 1870 :—

' In the first place, let me give you my congratulations on your safe return, and add those on the blessing you enjoy in having a son like Ferdinand. Thank you for letting me see his letter ; I could not resist showing it to my wife, and the reading of it affected us as much as every real pleasure does. I have always had a great opinion of his character ; his heart and his intellect are well balanced. But this letter surpassed my expectations as an expression of his childlike but already very mature nature.'

Ferdinand had chosen work which was entirely congenial to him, and made him financially independent from his nineteenth year. Though he had always lived in a large town and been his own master since he left school, he had led a singularly pure life. His innate purity and almost touching reverence for women, which was expressed in his whole attitude towards them, made him instinctively proof against low influences.

FELIX

Our father never saw him, but he gave him his name, calling him Felix after the ' Unforgettable.' [2] Indeed, the boy seemed predestined not only to be happy himself, but to make others happy. If ever a mother's hopes for

[1] Ferdinand served in the German army during the Franco-Prussian War, and returned with bad rheumatism. Ten years later, when serving with the Militia, he was attacked by severe rheumatic fever and taken to hospital in Berlin, where an unscrupulous doctor trusted him with morphia. It became a fatal temptation to him. In accesses of pain he became a slave to this drug. After many years of terrible suffering he met with a melancholy end. He had married young, and left six children, a daughter and five sons. Felix became consumptive in his nineteenth year, and died when he was twenty-four.

[2] Felix Mendelssohn.

her son were justified by brilliant gifts, a rare character, nobility, and kindness of heart, combined with a charming disposition and attractive appearance, my mother's surely were when they centred in him.

We all had our share of her love without partiality, but her relations to this youngest child, whom she had borne during the most sorrowful time of her life, were of a particularly tender kind. I became doubly aware of this when I read her letters, and it was only then that I fully realised her anguish when this son was attacked by consumption in his nineteenth year, and she had to watch him dying a lingering death.

Similarity of temperament drew them closely together. Felix speaks to her without restraint of everything that is of importance to him, and my mother's letters show her respect for his early maturity, her appreciation of his understanding of all her emotions and moods. Eugenie as a grown woman has received similarly unrestrained letters from her mother, but Eugenie the schoolgirl never. Not once did she let herself go to me when I was of Felix's age as she did to him.

She writes on May 11, to the boy who was not yet thirteen :—

' KARLSBAD, 11 *May* 1867.

' . . . I am writing to-day chiefly because of something which touches me very nearly. Grandmother and Ferdinand tell me that you are thinking of becoming a violinist. This would be a very serious step, more so than you may imagine. However good your work might be, if it were not quite outstanding, the part which the son of Robert Schumann would play in the world would be invidious. I would impress upon you that with your name you are justified in choosing a musical career only if you are a genius, and in addition work enormously hard. Although I am quite convinced that your talent is sufficient to afford you and others pleasure if you use it as an amateur (but even for this you must do hard work), I am equally sure that your gifts are not such as will carry you to the summits of art. I therefore beg you to think it well over, my beloved Felix. You have so many other gifts that you might choose almost any other career, and perhaps distinguish yourself in it (whatever it may be)—of course, always provided that you work very hard. This would give you a better position in the world than you would be likely to attain as a musician. . . . But to make quite sure both for your own sake and for mine, I will ask Herr Joachim to hear you play, and to let you stay with him for a couple of days when you come to Baden. He will be the best and most impartial judge. What do you think of this ? Write and tell me. . . .'

'BADEN-BADEN, 13 *August* 1867.

'MY DEAR FELIX,—I ought to be doing many things, but your letters have been such a joy to me that I must answer them myself and send you a kiss. Your good wishes arrived yesterday when we had just returned from our walk, and were a great surprise. How charming of you, my boy, to have thought of this ! [1] Here we feel about you as you in Berlin feel about us, for we often think of you and talk about you. We accompanied you with our thoughts on your whole journey and first day at school, which may have been hard enough for you. How I have felt our parting ! I could think of nothing else all that day. I thought it quite natural for me to say nice things about you to Herr Planer in my letter. Occasional little lapses of high spirits and thoughtlessness do not count when a person gives one so much pleasure as you, my little fellow, give to us. And in my pleasure I gratefully remember those to whom I and you owe so much. . . . We expect Julie back on the seventeenth, and are all looking forward to it ; we have missed her

---

[1] Her patron saint's day.

73

greatly. I miss you all so much when you are away from me ; you are the greatest happiness that my life affords, and I hope I shall live to see you all grow into useful and happy men and women.

'I am sorry to say that Elise will soon leave us. Fräulein A. has left for Hanover, and now Fräulein O., Marie's friend, is with us. Friedchen Wagner is coming soon, and Fräulein Leser will leave at the end of the month. Life is like the tide, in small things and in great, in joy and sorrow, arrival and parting. My motherly love alone remains firm for all eternity, and with that I embrace you, my dear Felix.—Your old

'MOTHER KLARA.'

' 10,000,000,000 kind messages from us all.

' You need only have a little tuck sewn in the sleeves of your shirts to make them shorter. Talk to Ferdinand about it.'

In 1868 Felix had been obliged to stay away from school for six months on account of his health. On January 20, 1869, he wrote to his mother :—

' . . . I am well otherwise, only I have to be careful, as there is now an icy wind as well as the great cold. I have to work very hard, but, although I am at it pretty steadily, I don't seem to get on very well, and my fear of not getting my remove at Easter is growing from week to week.'

His mother's answer to this was :—

' LONDON, 5 *February* 1869.

' . . . I should like to know the date of removes in your school, so that I may think of you with very special good wishes. But I want you to know one thing, my dear Lix : do not worry if you do not get your remove— one cannot go beyond human strength, and if you are sure that you have done your very best, you may rest satisfied. It was not your fault that you had to stay away from school, and if it has put you back a little, that will not be a great disaster, considering your abilities. The years at school seem long to you ; this feeling is shared by all ambitious people, who would like those years to speed up. But that cannot be done ; patient study is the only thing that will make them pass to advantage. . . . I must go to my work now, but my thoughts remain with you. You children are always near to my heart. Sometimes my anxieties are such a heavy burden that they weigh down the wings of my soul ; but when I bid hope return, the wings spread, and my pulses beat higher.

' Farewell, my own boy. Kiss Ferdinand from me, and let yourself be caught to the heart of your old

' MOTHER KLARA.'

' BADEN, 18 *June* 1869.

' MY DEAR FELIX,—I have had specially heavy expenses this summer, but that shall not prevent me from giving you the pleasure of coming to us, for you are a hard worker and this makes me happy. Come, and God bless you—but it must be third class. . . . I kiss you for your dear letters, but I cannot help giving you a slight hint at the same time. You do not always write quite natur-ally, but seem to take pleasure in a rather florid style, as though you were trying to be clever. But when the reader becomes conscious of this intention, a letter from a beloved person loses something of its freshness. . . .'

The letters referred to cannot be found. But a few months later he writes :—

' BERLIN, 10 *August* 1869.

' DEAR MAMMA !—Now I am back in Berlin after leaving Baden on Friday ; how soon the time there has passed, and how greatly I am longing for you and the others, wishing I were still with you ! There are moments of which one says they are the unhappiest of one's life ; this feeling is casting its shadow over me now. I am with you constantly, and my thoughts constantly turn like a compass away from my books and towards you, wondering what you are doing. I wish I could cry my fill, but I am afraid people would not be considerate enough not to make remarks about red eyes. There is no brook, either, to murmur comfort, no fir-tree with whispering branches, no rose to diffuse perfume, no flowery mead with pearly dew, no veiled mountains, no purple sunset. A grey sun is kissing a grey quadrangle's four grey walls, and there is no loving voice to say : Be of good cheer, Felix ! Look at your mother, who has suffered more than you, and yet time has softened her grief.

' I am turning a certain matter over and over in my mind, and my heart ever urges me towards music. I know there is much to be said against it, but I always return to it. I know that the career which I am about to choose is a difficult one, and that there are now a thousand musicians. But why should I not be the one thousand and first ? . . . What would happen if the sons of great men were always great men too ? There would be no distinction in being a great man. But there is something fine in the endeavour of a son of a great man to grasp his father's greatness and that of his art. . . . I am now anxious to know if you would dis-approve of my choosing this career. . . .'

' BERLIN, 3 *September* 1869.

' DEAR MAMMA !—I am writing chiefly in order to send you the prospectus of the proposed new school of music in Berlin, to which you had thought of sending me.[1] If the scheme is carried out, Berlin must soon be the rallying-point for classical music and all serious musicians.

[1] Königliche Hochschule für Musik.

FELIX SCHUMANN

IN HIS EIGHTEENTH YEAR

Those who are now turning up their noses in contempt will have to slink away ashamed and humbled. They say that there are already an enormous number of entries, no doubt because many advantages are offered besides the lessons. I have at last got the better of my scruples. Let me go my own way, dear Mother, and leave what comes of it to me and my fate. I am glad to have made up my mind, and half-hearted people will not affect me or turn me from my purpose. By Easter I shall have polished up my Kreutzer studies; do not worry about that any more than about my remove. I shall hardly be admitted to the piano class, as my technique is insufficient. I only wish I could save you the anxiety of where I am to live. But although in small things one may be guided by general principles, the latter must not be the outcome of narrow circumstances, especially when the career of a lifetime is at stake. I find it hard myself to realise that I must leave the people with whom I have lived six long, happy years; who have developed my mind, given me the first conscious impressions; to whom I am bound both by habit and gratitude, so that I shall always feel their debtor, for youth ever owes a debt which can never be repaid. I am like a polypus attached to a stern rock; torn from it, the ends of its tentacles cling to what it has so long embraced.

' I can imagine how deeply Klementine's death [1] must have grieved you. Fate has rarely sundered closer bonds, rarely left a greater void in the lives of fond relations, rarely called a warmer heart from this earth. But he would be ungrateful who should call the powers that directed this fate cruel, for she did not die in a strange country, but in her own home; not far from her dear ones, but in their arms; her ashes have been received by the soil of her own country, and rest near to those of her father and grandmother. Poor Grandmamma is

[1] Klementine Bargiel, our mother's half-sister.

77

terribly stricken, and so is Auntie ; they do not know how to bear the loss, how to go on living.

' Thus the decrees of fate turn a happy circle into a sad one, taking joy and gladness with them ; and while here the cypress is pressed on a dead brow, you will soon bind the myrtle into a bride's hair.[1]

' The funeral took place at five o'clock yesterday, and as everything was well arranged beforehand, the ceremony was really beautiful and touching, especially to me, who was playing the sad part of a mourner for the first time in my life. The procession started from the chapel of Holy Trinity cemetery, where stood the coffin, made of choice wood finely and gracefully fashioned and decorated with festoons of lovely laurel and white roses. Palms, cypress, and myrtle were arranged on either side ; at the head a platform had been erected for the officiating clergyman, the same who had confirmed her. His address was beautiful, simple and heartfelt, without rhetoric, which is always best. How one feels as though it would be good to be with the dead, unless one could restore them to life ! Then the coffin was carried very quietly to the grave. Many walked in the procession, but you will have heard about all that ; I am telling you because one feels the need of communicating what is constantly in one's heart. A very beautiful thing happened : a ray of sunshine suddenly broke through clouds and waked the song of a charming bird to a long-sustained, mournful tune. Many, many wreaths and flowers filled the grave, destined to become dust with her whom they covered. Auntie wept heartbreakingly : I tried to feel with her, for there is nothing more beautiful than to feel fully the sorrows of others, even though the sting may not immediately affect oneself.

' You will have heard that Ferdinand has moved again. For the moment his hope of a visit to you is rather in abeyance, but I wish above everything that after this

---

[1] Refers to Julie's wedding.

long time he could once more return to the delightful circle whose crown and centre is our dear Mamma. His constant isolation is becoming almost unbearable to him.

'Farewell, and give my warmest greeting to all.— Your loving   FELIX.'

'BERLIN, 28 *September* 1869.

'DEAR MAMMA !—The auspicious day is over.[1] Ferdinand gave me the token of your love in the morning, and I thank you a thousand, thousand times for it. The ring has given me great pleasure, and when I saw it I thought at once : Surely Marie has helped to choose it. It shows her taste in any case, which is mine also ; the dull gold sets off the blue stone beautifully ; in short, I like it so much that my finger has grown fat in the middle with pleasure, and the ring will not come off. . . .

'As to the confirmation service, it was very beautiful. Ferdinand, Aunt Caecilie, and Frau Planer with her daughter went to the church with me. I felt a little nervous at first, but it does one good to get out of the ordinary everyday mood occasionally into a more exalted one in which, instead of looking beneath oneself at ordinary human occupations, one looks above with pure emotions to something indescribably beautiful and profound. But it is fortunate also that moods such as these do not occur often ; for those who desire wings to hover above the ordinary life, and imagine that they are guided by some ideal, usually drop down wearily to earth, and their wings are plucked off, if not by Cupid then by another. When we had made our vow, we went up to the altar in groups of three or four, where we knelt on the steps, and the clergyman, laying his hands on our heads in turn, spoke over each of us a quotation from the Bible to remember for our lifetime. I thought of Goethe's " Alexis " when he says : " Then an honoured

---

[1] His confirmation.

79

father laid his hand upon my curly head in blessing ; a careful mother gave into my hand a well-stocked bundle. Return happily, they cried, happy and rich."

' Yes, dear Mamma, you too are saying loving words like these, and their fulfilment rests chiefly with me. I have become convinced of one thing which has always struck me so much in the Greeks, viz. that religion is the background on which politics, science, and art rest : to them it imparts vitality and maturity ; they are involved in its ruin when, as so often happens, religion is deliberately shattered and deprived of its sanctity. Its vital nerves, like the nerves and muscles of our body, run invisibly beneath our social structure ; mind and heart only can appreciate their significance, which is as deep now as it was in ancient times. And what a beautiful example and incentive I have in you ! You never talk about religion, do not often go to church or observe outward forms of that kind, but what need for that ? It is in actions that the true character reveals itself, and as far as my small understanding can measure your actions they inspire me with deep admiration, respect, love, and the zeal to show myself worthy of such a mother.

' Next Sunday I shall go to my first Communion, which will put the seal on my confirmation. . . . Now I will tell you that I got my report yesterday ; I did not think it necessary to send it, on account of the heavy postage. My work and progress, conduct and attention, are said to have been satisfactory on the whole, and I was rewarded to-day by an undeserved prize. I had not expected it, and am annoyed about it, because other pupils deserve it more. You will say that the teachers are sure to be just. Bon ! But in this case they are not, and as a punishment for me the prize consisted in Lessing's works, which you had already given me, and that is another annoyance. I would like to know if I might give one of the two, *e.g.* your present, to Ferdinand ?

The prize will, however, make me try to be worthy of it next term. I am too excited to write properly ; forgive me.—Love to all. YOUR FELIX.'

Though unwillingly, our mother had given way to Felix's choice of a musical career, on condition that he stayed out his time at school. This was a bitter disappointment to him, and in the first rush of emotions he vented his resentment on the friends with whom he was living. A series of conflicts followed with his old master, Professor Planer, to whom he really was devoted.

Some passages in the next letter refer to this :—

' BERLIN, 26 *December* 1869.

' DEAR MAMMA !—Your Felix, until now a most unbearable Felix, has turned over a new leaf. It is not only that his bearing is improved, though every one says that he has grown several inches since the Lady his Mother has been here ; not only that he heaps books around himself, undecided where to begin to make himself more stupid than he is ; not the flying lapels of his jacket which reveal the gold watch-chain of a proud gentleman, his violet suit, kid-gloved hands, and handsome studs ; not only that he wastes his substance unreasonably on gingerbread and raisins . . . a little of all this combined has worked the change, but chiefly the consciousness of how good every one has been to him.

' You will say : Have we not always been good to you ? But that is just it ! The human eye is often blind and dull when it has to face something that hurts for the moment. We will not believe in the kernel until we hold the shell in our hand. It is bad to see so late how much one has been loved, how careless and ungrateful one has been. But now I will be ungrateful no longer, neither towards Providence nor you. Woe to him whose remorse, like furies, will torment a too-forgetful mind ! I wonder what the word " thankful " really means ? I have not read a philosophical treatise on it, but I expect it means " thinking of." I will not expound this, as I do not care to dig for the root of every word or dissect it. Whatever it may really mean, I know that I am, and always shall be, thankful to you with all my heart. I am specially glad of the Shakespeare, which was quite a surprise. I should have written yesterday, but going to church took up the best part of the morning. It was badly heated, and when one's feet are very cold they unfortunately freeze one's heart. Thank dear Marie from me for the charming studs. Minzlein's taste, which is mine too, showed in those studs. Herr Planer, who gave me many presents, sends his kindest regards ; Fräulein Planer many thanks. These are all the messages.

'Your Felix.'

'Vienna, 28 *December* 1869.

'My beloved Felix,—You have rejoiced my heart with your letters, especially the last one, which shows me that you are getting the better of your depression. I can quite feel with you how hard it is to give up a favourite idea, but your whole future is at stake, and I do not demand renunciation but only postponement. Classics, which now seem unnecessary to you, will later on be an advantage, both mentally and as regards your social position. Thorough culture secures a good reception in every circle ; you will be looked upon not only as an artist, but as a cultured man.

'London, 26 *February* 1870.

' . . . I am again in full work here ; my reception is extraordinary, but I have great exertions, which I can stand less well now, and if I should come again next year I shall have to do less. It is always a great joy to me to play with Joachim and Piatti, but this is the only thing that makes musical life here bearable. It makes up for many other things which have to be endured because they cannot be avoided. When I see how the artists here work from morning till night, that art is to them merely a means of making money, I feel quite sad at the thought, " What has become of your ideals ? " I feel how fortunate I am in going to my work fresh in mind and heart, and I will preserve this good fortune even at the cost of remaining a poor musician. . . .'

' BERLIN, 20 *June* 1870.

' DEAR MAMMA !—To my gratitude for your last long and longed-for letter I add a request which I can only put before you with some anxiety. But first of all I will answer some things in your letter which I cannot pass over. I see that you have taken a part of my letter differently from what I meant. I cannot conceive how it could annoy you when I wrote that I was taking life more seriously now. Does that necessarily mean that I am complaining of not having all I want, or something of the sort ? . . . Is it not sad and bitter enough to know that a brother is for ever doomed to unhappiness ? Is not that a bitter drop in the cup of all joy ? And even if he were not my brother, is it not unhappiness enough to know that you are always sorrowful, to see you thus ? I think when one gets older one is less apt to invariably make personal happiness or unhappiness the starting-point for everything ; one's outlook becomes larger, and one sees the clouds on the horizon. May Heaven dispel them !

' I have been a great expense to you this year, and have irritated you so much with my last letter that I can only ask in fear and trembling whether you are willing to let me come home for the holidays, which are beginning on July 9? I am afraid you will say, " He does not deserve it " ; but please let me hear soon, so that I can get over the shock. I have been looking forward so long to the coming weeks ; when I was depressed I thought of them, and mind and heart, those heavy, dull things, felt refreshed.'

83

' BADEN, 22 *June* 1870.

'MY DEAR LIX,—I received your letter yesterday together with Ferdinand's, which was a great shock to us. Poor Ludwig's fate is terrible ; I can find no words for grief such as this—it tears my heart. I could not bear it at all, if I did not feel that I owe it to you to pull myself together. If God would only take the poor boy to Himself ! He suffers while he is still so young and life owes him everything, and I, nearly at the end of mine, can still enjoy nature and all the things that are left to me.

' Oh, my dear boy, never give me trouble ; this one is so great that it is almost unbearable. My dearest hopes are centred in you, and I am sure you will become a useful member of human society if you fight against the faults which prevent you from doing your duty, especially your obstinacy. We can overcome much if we try, and I am sure you mean to try, if only for love of me.

' You know how much we too are looking forward to your holidays, and thank God I can afford to let you come ; but it must be third-class, dear boy ! Take a cushion or rug with you. . . .'

Felix to his Mother.

' BERLIN, 26 *June* 1870.

' . . . when I came to the end of your letter, new life seemed to flow through my veins. I had just pushed aside some work, too tired and bothered to go on with it. I took it up again, pulled myself together, clenched my fists and said : " I will do it, and it shall be done." . . .'

And it was done. Felix, whose inclinations had turned him from school routine and books, firmly took them up again, and how well he did his duty the following words from his mother from Baden, October 14, 1870, show : ' Dearest Lix, I am returning your report, and give you a kiss for this and many other things ' ; and a letter from—

BROTHERS AND SISTERS

' LONDON, 7 *April* 1871.

' MY MUCH-BELOVED LIX,—Best wishes from me and us all for your remove, and a warm kiss, which you will no doubt gladly put up with though you are an Upper Form boy. This last year at school too will pass, and then a new life will begin for you. May you be taking the right course, and the one most satisfactory to you ; what I can do towards it I will. . . . I kiss you for your letters, too, my dear boy ; they are always such a true pleasure to me. . . .

' You need not be afraid of my being away during your holidays. I trust we shall spend them together, and perhaps we may get our wish and see Ferdinand too. . . . My heart beats higher when I think of Germany, where, God granting, I shall soon return. It is a curious thing : we are greatly spoilt here, the Burnands antici-pate our smallest wishes, yet my longing for German soil, German speech, apart from all that is dear to me there, is growing stronger every hour. It gives me pure joy when all I hear and see around me is German once more. But this does not make me ungrateful towards the English, who welcome and receive me each time with so much love. Now I will say farewell to you, my beloved Lix, and embrace you with all my heart. I wish you could feel how much my thoughts are with you, how my fond-est hopes are centred in you ! Our poor Ludwig, too, then comes into my mind, and my heart bleeds for him. It is a long time since I received a doctor's report about him.—Your old devoted

' MOTHER KLARA.'

Meanwhile the doctors had given their opinion that Felix was not strong enough for the career of an instru-mentalist. He had to renounce his hopes of becoming a musician, and it was decided that he should finish his schooling and study law. Before he had attained his nineteenth year he passed brilliantly into the University. His examination papers had been handed in when he wrote as follows to his mother :—

' 15 *March* 1872.

' . . . I should have written sooner, had I not been anxious to wait till after the Viva. Now this is happily over, or rather it never took place, for they let me off.'

He went to Heidelberg as a student of law, happy and full of hope. I saw him a few weeks later, for the first time since he had outgrown his boyhood. A tall, handsome youth in the full rig-out of a German undergraduate, riding-whip in hand, he met me on the platform. He had the air of one who was about to conquer the world. Of the little brother, the sensitive boy, there remained only the blue eyes and shock of fair hair escaping from his cap and falling across his forehead. After nine years of severest discipline he revelled in the freedom of a student's life. He was reading the Pandects in Heidelberg, as his father had done before him, and occupied himself with literary studies. He had taught himself a fair amount of Italian and Spanish while he was at school ; now he translated Moore's and Burns's poems, wrote poetry himself, played the violin, joined the orchestra of the ' Museum,' playing second fiddle, roamed mountains and woods, rowed, went to inns and fooled about, but always frankly confessed his pranks to his mother.

I do not think that he had decided upon a definite career at the time. He once wrote :—

' 'Twould become me ill
   To live on my father's fame.
   Myself to make me a name,
That is my will.'

He was expected to do well whatever he might ultimately choose to take up ; great hopes were founded on him. All our friends near and far took an interest in his development. Brahms once told our mother, ' I don't know how I should contain myself with happiness if I had a son like Felix.' We all loved him indescribably, and were proud of him. He was so genuine, full of high aspirations, without pettiness : the true child of his parents. I see him before me coming to us on Sundays or during the vacations, always dressed in light grey. In spite of the best intentions to save his mother's purse, his choice would invariably fall on the nicest and most expensive materials. How happy he was with us ! Now quiet and thoughtful, now keenly observant and witty ; always charming, and always ready for fun. I can hear his laugh, when Marie in private theatricals came on the stage dressed as a student, in a performance of Körner's ' Watchman,' in which the boys and girls from the next cottage took part. I would close his memoir on the note of that laughter and remember him thus ; I would take leave of the beloved form in all the glory of youth, before the cold hand of fate touched him and destroyed all his hopes and all ours. What need to lift the veil from five years of great suffering, when the inexorable disease cut off his life with cruel deliberation ? He, a patient sufferer, has long been released, has seen the light and been answered ; while we, still tied here, still ask : Why ? From the unanswerable I turn to the memory of the short time we spent together with this brother, young and hopeful, lending brightness to our lives. He, too, had the comfort of which he once wrote when a dear relative died. He ' did not die in a strange country, but in his home ; not far from his loved ones, but in their arms ; his ashes rest in the soil of his country.'

From a number of poems by Felix Schumann the following three have been selected, which we print in a prose translation by Mr. R. C. Trevelyan, who has closely followed the original text. The first of these is well known through Brahms's composition, 'Meine Liebe ist grün.' The third is Felix Schumann's last.

I

My love is green as the lilac bush, and my beloved is fair as the sun, that shines down upon the lilac bush and fills it with fragrance and with rapture.

My soul has the wings of a nightingale, and sways amid the blossoming lilac, and, drunk with the scent, carols and sings many love-intoxicated songs.

II. DREAMS, LOVELY COMFORTERS

Thanks be to thee, God of Dreams, thou who didst fill with lovely images the hours of sleep so rarely granted me. Beautiful forms, sinuous and graceful, I beheld approach me, surround me, and kiss my forehead, whispering tenderly, ' Sorrow not, for we love thee ! '

What I enjoyed in dream, did I enjoy it less than what with waking senses I feel and think ? Is the scent of the flower less real than leaves and petals ; the shining of eyes, the melody of the voice, less real than neck and bosom ? Less real the songs of the poet than the deeds of his heroes ? He who is denied enjoyment of the day's sunny delights must content himself with images of dreams. Through winter's clouds and mists I see those forms shine and smile ; in the moment when anguish threatens I hear them whisper, ' Sorrow not, for we love thee ! '

III. DESPAIR

I held up to Heaven the cup of misery, filled to the brim, and prayed, ' Pour down but one drop of joy, but one drop of happiness, into the bitter bowl.' Then there fell down like a shooting-star a drop that promised fulfilment of all the wishes I ever cherished.

But, alas ! the cup overflowed, and with it ran down that drop of heavenly dew.

O miserable, betrayed heart of man !

EUGENIE SCHUMANN
IN HER EIGHTEENTH YEAR

Last of all :—

EUGENIE

What is to be said for her? She had many shortcomings, and never cared much for herself; but as you all loved her so much, there must have been some good in her. If I could have you all with me once more, how much better should I understand you, how much more should I love you ! We all have suffered much, for the sorrows of one were the sorrows of all. But it was a beautiful thing, this love for each other, our common love for our parents and the common desire to show ourselves worthy of them.

OUR MOTHER

AND what shall I say of her, the sun that spread light and warmth on our lives, our Mother ?

In the summer of 1869 she was in her fiftieth year, of little more than medium height, but so well made that she seemed tall. All her movements were quick without being hurried. When she came into a room, it always seemed as if a breeze were stirring everything about her ; the dull room suddenly became full of animation and sunshine.

Many portraits of her have made her features familiar; yet what mechanical apparatus, what pencil, could render the mind and soul that animated these features, their mobility and changing colour ? The best portrait-painter of the time confessed that it was impossible to fix the total impression of her personality on canvas, complaining that the aspect it presented would often change entirely within one sitting, within a few minutes even. Two wonderful sketches made by him within a few hours are both like her, yet entirely different from each other. Perfect repose and utmost animation dwelt closely together. Her forehead, framed by ample, smooth, dark hair, expressed clarity and purity of thought, but at the same time reflected her every mood. How often I have marvelled at this harmony when I saw clouds, light or heavy, pass across it ! Even in her old age her forehead remained smooth ; only the closest inspection showed a hairbreadth of furrow running across. The oval cheeks were still more mobile ; annoyance or sorrow caused the muscles to slacken at once, and she would then suddenly look old and suffering. Pleasant sensations rejuvenated her with equal rapidity.

How can I describe her eyes ? They were stars which inevitably attracted every one who came within the orbit of their light. The Artist-Creator had mixed many colours to a shade of indescribable warmth and softness, and added a sheen of silver over all. These eyes had shed many tears without losing their brilliance. One never tired of looking into their depths to see a steady growth and deepening of the spirit reveal itself more and more gloriously. No one on whom they have rested could have forgotten the tale they told of her true kindness of heart, her infinite benevolence. They searched and understood you at a glance, they ' wrapped you round,' as a dear friend once said. When the conversation turned on art, on noble qualities, on beauties of nature, they looked as though she could see into a world more beautiful than this.

Her mouth, which ever spoke lovingly and tenderly to us, expressed in its lines a firm character. A shade of irony would sometimes steal into the corners of the lips which closed lightly upon each other. Her voice was sympathetic and mellow ; we children loved her slight lisp. Her Saxon dialect gave rise to a great deal of teasing, when for instance she would say ' Gohannes ' instead of Johannes.

No other feature betrayed as her hands did what my mother had accomplished and suffered. They were supple and large—she played tenths from the wrist ; the fingers tapered slightly ; the thumb was beautifully curved, and the little finger, probably through early training, very little shorter than the third. Though the wrist was so strong, it was delicately built, and the gradual rounding of her arm was beautiful. Innumerable fine lines had engraved themselves upon these hands and fingers which were the medium which conveyed art into life, life into art. When she grew older, her hand resembled Goethe's more and more, so that, seeing a cast of his, people exclaimed, 'That is Frau Schumann's hand!'

From her childhood she had been accustomed to take care of her hands. She was never allowed to lift any weight, and had to renounce every occupation which might have induced the slightest stiffness; she gave up the crocheting of handsome bedspreads, which had been a favourite pastime of hers during the afternoon tea-hour. Whenever she was in the garden she wore gloves with the tips cut off. I never could help regretting the decapitation of handsome suèdes. One of the few pieces of needlework which my mother ever did was the stitching round of the cut fingers of these gloves, when she would use a coarse needle and a very long thread.

If I were asked to describe the general impression of her personality, I would say that she was the perfection of womanhood, of motherhood and humanity. She was an incarnation of the saying of Goethe :

' Only from perfect strength shines forth an inner grace.'

When I looked at her coming towards me from a distance, I seemed to see a halo of soft light surrounding her. Later on, when I heard Mrs. Besant speak of the ' aura ' which surrounds a person and becomes more distinct with spiritual growth, I could not help feeling that there was some truth in this, when I remembered my mother.

I looked up to her with great love, but also with awe. She was so far above the poor undeveloped schoolgirl, that I could not at first and for a long time get over a feeling of remoteness and timidity. Her own development had been so extraordinary that she probably had no idea of the state of mind of a quite ordinary human being. Predestined by nature for art, she had been fortunate in having a father who recognised this quite early, and ordered her life wisely and firmly from her

childhood, so that she could live exclusively for high
ideals. She had not had more instruction than was
absolutely necessary, had never been to a boarding-
school, and from her tenth year onwards she had lived
under the eye of the public, grown up under it, and
developed in constant intercourse with eminent men and
women of the world. At thirteen she was grown up,
and already passionately devoted to our father. A few
years later she was at the zenith of her fame as Klara
Wieck, and of happiness because beloved by the friend
of her childhood. I was now of the age she had been
then, and what had my life contained so far? I had
accomplished nothing. I had had good instructors and
acquired a certain amount of knowledge, but knew
nothing, absolutely nothing, of life, not even of the bonds
of family life. I had lived among strangers longer than
any of my brothers and sisters. Now I was expected to
fit myself into my family, and I confess that I found it
difficult. I missed my companions, our common lessons
and games. Domestic work was irksome to me, and I
demurred at my older sisters' superiority. My mother
seemed to me severe, because undoubtedly she fixed the
highest standards for our industry, sense of duty, regard
for the feelings of others, and self-command. Yet since
she herself set so great an example, who could have
resented her demands? She measured her own conduct
by these standards in great and in small things. To know
what was right and to do it was one and the same impulse
with her. I have never known her hesitate, even in the
face of great sacrifices. She once found me reading
Hilty's *Happiness*, and asked me whether it was a good
book? I read her a few passages, and she said, ' I don't
understand a word of it, but happiness seems to me a very
simple thing. You need only do your duty under all
circumstances.'

She had drained the cup of sorrow to the last drop, but
her genius gave her strength to turn its bitterness into

sweetness, and to attain to the greatest human perfection. Having raised her to be a priestess of art, her genius demanded the harmonious perfecting of all her qualities of mind, heart, and soul. Nature's gifts had been lavish ; her own task was to dispose of these gifts, to mould and balance them well, to bring full self-assertion into harmony with the recognition of the rights of others.

I do not know whether this had been a difficult task for my mother, whether she had had to struggle against temperamental faults. She once exhorted me to correct a certain fault, and when I told her I was too old to change she smiled and answered, ' I am much older than you, yet I am constantly correcting myself.' And when I looked at her incredulously, she continued : ' Perhaps you will remember that I was apt to lose my temper. When your sister Julie grew up, I saw that she too had a temper, and I said to myself, " Unless one of us changes, we shall be very unhappy together ; Julie is young and very delicate, I am older and stronger, it is I who must change." And you will admit that I succeeded ; you do not see me give way to temper now,' she concluded.

Darling, wonderful Mother ! I take for granted what you told me, but it has always seemed to me as though it were easy to you to tread lightly where others stumbled on life's stony paths—easy as the perfection of your art. Where we toiled along, you flew ; there was an *élan*, a spontaneity, in all you did which lent indescribable fascination to daily life with you.

There were times, indeed, when she suffered from deep depression, or was angry or annoyed at something. But she never vented these feelings on her surroundings, never gave way to moodiness, sulkiness, or mere irritability. She herself suffered at those times, but she was kind and patient to others. Her greatness consisted in this perfect self-control, and I would go so far as to say that it made a Christian of my mother in the truest sense,

94

Photograph Elliott & Fry.

CLARA SCHUMANN

though she did not realise it herself. Infinite benevolence was the keynote of her relations to all human beings ; I have often marvelled at her bringing it into harmony with strong sympathies and antipathies, keen observation and unerring judgment. Her kindness embraced all with whom she came in contact, without regard to station.

We did not by any means like all the people whom she admitted into the circle of her acquaintances. We said on one occasion, ' Mamma, how can you be friends with these people and be so nice to them ? They are not really loyal to you, and only want to boast of knowing a celebrity.' And she said, ' You may be right, but they have good qualities for which I respect them. The husband is clever and a good worker in his profession, and she is a very good wife and mother, and her life is not quite easy.'

When we begged her to get rid of an unsympathetic pupil, who was moreover without musical gifts, she said, ' It is not her fault that she has no talent or personal charm, but she is industrious and full of zeal, has no one belonging to her, and will have to earn her living.' She never said things like these in a superior tone, or as if she wanted to teach us a lesson. They came quite spontaneously, as though it were the most natural thing to say. She gave her sympathy generously, advised and helped where she could—and she somehow usually could ; she was lenient towards faults, and forgave easily. Only where she found meanness of character she turned away once and for ever.

She was above all littleness herself, incapable of jealousy in art or in life. She would have every one enjoy what was his, and judged every merit, every person without prejudice, even when love or admiration might have been expected to bias her. Indeed, she exacted most where she loved most.

Her friend, Professor Engelmann, once said to me :

' Do you know what I take to be the reason for your mother's enormous influence in the world ? It is the absolute integrity of her judgment. When we want in the Society of Musicians to have an opinion on the merits of an artist or new music, we ask your mother. She is always absolutely impartial ; others are influenced by circumstances or personal relations.' And truly, when I try to think of a single prejudice of hers against persons, things, or ideas, I can find none. She met every new phenomenon in art or in life with perfect open-mindedness. If on inspection she found it pernicious, she turned her back on it without hesitation ; but when she found it good, no matter whence it came, she drew it into her life and held it there.

This, then, was my mother who now, with infinite love and patience, tried to draw me also towards herself. She never wearied of teaching, helping, pardoning me. Being ever industrious herself, she expected the same of us ; she could not bear to see us idle during that part of the day which was set apart for work. ' Make use of minutes,' she said ; ' they are irretrievable.' When she found me in the dining-room waiting for dinner, she said that I ought to make use of the time by memorising some piece of music. She was an early riser, in spite of frequent bad nights, and worked almost uninterruptedly between breakfast and mid-day. Her large correspondence took up several hours daily, and she spent about two hours at the piano. When she went into her room after breakfast, the first thing she did was to open the piano, one of us dusted it, and it remained open all day. She usually played for an hour after breakfast, and again in the late afternoon towards twilight. This was the hour when her glorious improvisations revealed to us feelings which she did not put into words. Often though she spoke to us of her childhood and the early days of her love, she hardly ever alluded to the tragic times which preceded our father's death. But the strains of her music during these twilight hours spoke of all the grief she had borne and the heroism with which she had endured it. She never indulged in grief ; she sought and found consolation in music, and when she returned to the family circle she at once shared our interests, and enjoyed what life had to offer her of good and pleasant things.

I was now expected to take my share of the lighter domestic work, and each hour of the day had its regular occupation. My mother was anxious that I should continue the studies which I had begun at school. She also wished me to practise for three hours daily. I no longer was to be my sister's pupil ; she herself taught me twice a week for an hour in the mornings. She kept to these hours with the greatest regularity, no matter what demands were made upon her.

I remember my first lesson most distinctly. It began, like all the subsequent ones, with scales and arpeggios, and the first Study from· Czerny's School of Velocity followed. I played a page of it, then my mother said, ' That is all right so far, but don't you think chords sound much nicer like this ? ' She played the first eight bars from the wrist with all the notes of equal strength, forte, yet exquisitely mellow in tone, never stiffening the wrist for an instant, and knitting the chords rhythmically together so that the simple piece suddenly took on life and character. It was a revelation to me ; my feeling for beauty of touch and rhythm was stirred into life from that moment.

The study was followed by the Bach fugue in E minor from vol. i. of the ' Wohltemporierte Klavier.' I learnt strict legato and the subtle shading of rhythm in this. My mother took endless trouble with the first few bars ; but when these had been mastered, the fugue became easy, and I soon learnt to play it well enough to make it a pleasure to myself.

Beethoven formed the nucleus of every lesson. I

97

studied one sonata after another with great thoroughness ; she did not let the smallest inexactitude pass. What had been written was sacred to her. ' Do you think Beethoven would have taken the trouble to write all this notation, dots, ties, crotchets here, quavers there, if he had meant it to be otherwise ? And don't you hear for yourself that it must be so, and could not be anything else ? ' She laid stress on phrasing and shading, on a beautiful crescendo and the still more difficult diminuendo, on energetic accentuation without hardness, working up to a climax, and a thousand subtleties, in the sonatas. I understood her, but complete mastery of everything required years of study.

' And now we must work at some of Papa's music,' she said, when we had gone through the first movement of Beethoven's Sonata, op. 10, in D major, as far as the working-out section ; ' and I would like to start you with the ' " Jugend Album." ' So we took each of these little gems one by one in their proper order, and I remember every word the beloved teacher said about them. These pieces would teach me rhythm and characterisation ; underlying ideas I might supply myself. ' Whatever your father did, saw, read, would at once shape itself into music. When he read poetry, resting on the sofa after dinner, it turned into songs. When he saw you children at play, little pieces of music grew out of your games. While he was writing down the " Humoresque," some acrobats came along and performed in front of our house ; imperceptibly the music they made stole into the composition. He was always quite unconscious of these inspirations ; it would be foolish to think that he had used them intentionally as an incentive. He invented their titles after they were finished. These are quite characteristic, and might help in the interpretation, but they are not necessary.' When I asked her what the three little asterisks at the head of Nos. 21, 26, and 30 meant, she said with a tender look that he might have meant the thoughts of parents about their children.

The first piece I learnt was ' Armes Waisenkind,' and my mother explained it to me like this :—

' This is a theme of eight bars divided into twice four. The second four are a repetition of the first, all but the ending, which leads back to the tonic, while the first four end on the dominant. In a case like that you must vary the dynamics of the second four bars from those of the first, either shade them more strongly or more softly, but end them as strongly as you began the piece. Where the entire eight bars are repeated, play them exactly like the first time. If they are again repeated in the course of the piece, shade them differently the third time. In this " Armes Waisenkind " I should play the last repetition softly, graduating it to a pianissimo.'

She taught me this little piece with the greatest patience, and according to this rule, which helped me to understand and interpret other pieces where it applied.

Of the ' Jägerliedchen,' No. 7, she said, ' I can see the whole hunt before me, horns blowing, horses prancing, the hunters arriving from all sides.' Where the middle part is marked piano she said, ' The startled deer are flying into the bushes.' Four bars from the end, where the F unexpectedly becomes a G, she said, ' A bugler's note has cracked ; you will have heard the horns in the orchestra do that sometimes.'

Of the ' Fröhlicher Landmann ' she said that the father was at first singing alone ; his little son joins him in the middle part. Neither this nor the ' Schnitterlied ' should be played too fast : ' Look at peasants doing their work ; you will find that they never hurry themselves, not even in their dances.'

In ' Knecht Ruprecht ' Santa Claus could be heard stumbling upstairs knocking his staff on each step. In the middle part the trembling children hide, the old saint speaks encouragingly to them, empties his sack, and stumps downstairs again.

With No. 9, ' Lustig,' and No. 13, ' Mai, lieber Mai,' my mother took untold trouble. It was long before I played every tie, every portamento, every bit of phrasing as it was meant. She gave me no rest, and I am grateful to her to this day, for these pieces are truly enjoyable only when the minutest detail is observed.

In the ' Kleiner Morgenwanderer ' she taught me to play the chords as though I were lifting my feet in marching, not quite legato, and I felt at once that this gave the right character to the piece. She thought that the little wanderer was rather depressed in the beginning of the second part, at the thought of leaving home, but soon relieved his feelings with a yodel and walked on bravely, until the village was lost to his sight and he only heard the church bells ringing. I had to practise the slow diminuendo of these, as also the diminuendo of the hoofs in ' Reiterstück,' No. 23, for a long time before Mamma was satisfied. In the latter piece it was all the more difficult as the diminuendo already starts piano.

In ' Ländliches Lied,' No. 20, clearly a few girls only were singing at first ; then a mixed chorus of boys and girls joins them. At the beginning of the second part one girl is singing a solo, and at the return of the first theme ' one of the boys accompanies her on a reed pipe which he has just cut for himself.'

' Mignon ' was one of her favourites, and she taught it me with so much love that it became my favourite too. I was always looking forward to the fourth and third bars from the end, where careful shading will quite naturally give the intended significance to the dissonance.

Last of all I studied the ' Matrosenlied,' No. 37. I do not remember if I saw in it at the time all that my mother did ; but when I play it now I see before me, as in a picture, the infinite loneliness and melancholy of the sea, the watch's call, the heavy tread of sailors, their ponderous dance.

Explanations of this kind were very helpful to me. I remember the sforzati, which I played meaninglessly and, as my mother said, 'anæmically,' in 'Wilder Reiter,' No. 8. 'When a breakneck rider gallops about the room, he knocks his hobby-horse against chairs and tables.' Suddenly not only could I play these sforzati, but the idea of sforzato altogether, the suddenness with which it appears between the two less powerful notes, became once and for all clear to me and easy to execute. But it must not be thought that my mother was at all lavish with picturesque illustrations of this kind. She only gave them where she thought that they would help with the interpretation, and sometimes with no intention to instruct, simply because these images were a pleasure to herself. Later in life I once asked her whether all music conveyed pictures to her, and she said, 'Yes; and the older I grow, the more.'

But, as I have said, she never insisted on definite images, and never repeated them, but left it to the pupils to adopt as much of them as they liked.

With regard to fingering my mother restricted her annotations as much as possible, chiefly to tie-fingering. She disapproved of fingered editions, and held that one should have acquired the right feeling for fingering through study of scales, arpeggios, and other exercises. She also did not approve of otherwise annotated editions, and unwillingly consented, after an argument with Brahms, to my using Czerny's edition of Bach's fugues. Brahms had advised it as saving me trouble, because its ample fingering facilitates the division of the parts between the two hands, which otherwise has to be picked out laboriously. He said I need not pay attention to the other annotations, of which he too disapproved. When I became independent in my ideas and had gained experience in teaching, I inclined to my mother's view.

I found that pupils are quite sufficiently disinclined to pay attention to annotation, even where it is an integral part of the composition, and hesitated to add to it in any way.

My mother expected a good deal of me at first : a new study, a Bach fugue and prelude, part of a Beethoven sonata, and a Schumann or Chopin piece for every lesson, or at least once a week. But she soon saw that she must lower her standard. As I had only had an hour's daily practice at school, and probably had not even employed that to the best advantage, I had no technique. When I was at Wolfenbüttel I had once asked my mother's permission to practise for two hours. But she had refused, as she was anxious that I should get a good general education first of all. I have already mentioned that she had only had such instruction in her youth as was absolutely necessary, and she therefore wished us to have better advantages. How glad and proud she was when she found us knowing things which she had never learnt ! And we—how gladly we on our part would have given all our acquired knowledge for a breath of that genius which had enriched and consecrated our parents' lives !

But if my achievements were modest, Mamma's patience was unlimited, and every small improvement was generously praised. After the lesson she gave me a kiss and dismissed me, when I took myself and my music out of her room with a light heart.

OUR FRIENDS

O N the whole, our mode of life remained what I have described it as having been during the years of my childhood. Only Julie and Ludwig were at home besides Marie and myself at the beginning of this summer. Julie had returned engaged to be married. She had already dropped hints in her letters to me, and as soon as we were alone for a few minutes her ' petite confidente,' now grown up, was let into the secret. The engagement was not yet made public because her *fiancé*, Count Victor Radicati di Marmorito, the scion of an old Piedmontese family, a widower, and father of two little girls, was a Roman Catholic, and many difficulties had to be overcome first. It was a trying time for Julie, but she bore it with self-possession, and continued to brighten our lives with her sunny disposition. My mother's diary of 1869 often refers to Julie's charming ways and loving thought for her. All her life she had been passionately devoted to our mother. About a year before she died she confided to me that the moment of supreme happiness in her life had been when as a girl of eleven she had met our mother unexpectedly in the street, not knowing that she had arrived in Berlin.

While Marie was the daughter who bore the brunt of responsibilities for the household, Julie sought to adorn her mother's life with a thousand little loving-kindnesses. It was she who prepared her chocolate in the morning with great care and took it up to her room, she who anticipated each little need of hers, who put fresh flowers round our parents' portraits on memorial days. During this particular summer she undertook yet another duty.

She and my mother met daily an hour before dinner in the arbour near the Oos, and my mother, who never ceased to instruct herself, read French with her. The *Histoire d'un Conscrit de 1813*, by Erckmann-Chatrian, had been selected ; the pupil wrote down words and learnt them by heart for the next lesson.

Julie often gave way to the most delightful high spirits, and had not forgotten how to make grimaces : for example, on one occasion, when a well-known Italian singer, who afterwards married a famous prima-donna, had taken the house opposite to ours for the season. After our dinner Mamma usually opened the window of the dining-room, and we stood round her to see what was passing up and down the village street. The singer would then immediately appear on the balcony with his companions and stare across in a way to which we objected, but we did not know how to deal with the annoyance. When Julie joined us at the window for the first time and saw the inquisitive party, she dropped them a deep curtsy, but at the same time—oh, horror !— put her fingers to her nose and gave the tip of her tongue fair play. The result was instantaneous. For a moment the party stood as though frozen to the ground, then beat a hasty retreat and were seen no more.

At that time Baden-Baden was a meeting-place for famous and interesting people from all parts of the world. We did not entertain on a large scale, partly because my mother needed rest during the summer, and partly because our circumstances forbade the expense. Three of us were entirely dependent on my mother ; Felix was still at school. All these expenses had to be met, and what she could save she put aside for the future. Nevertheless, there was much animated social intercourse at our cottage, and a constant coming and going. The approach to my mother's room was by a rather dark passage with three treacherous steps ; even our intimate friends never got quite accustomed to them, and would sometimes come down head foremost, when we all ran shouting to the rescue. When the door was opened, the visitor entered a bright, cheerful room. Three windows in a line looked out upon the vine-covered veranda and well-tended little garden, the rapid Oos and the high plane-trees beyond. The grand piano stood along the wall opposite the windows. The wallpaper, grey with a little gold, had been carefully selected by Mamma and Marie to set off our beautiful prints to the best advantage. Casts of the Apollo of Belvedere and the Venus of Milo adorned the corners. The sofa stood along the broad wall opposite the folding doors which led into the adjoining smaller room, and the visitor who was sitting on it had a full view of a life-size portrait of his hostess painted by Sohn.

These rooms were visited by all the eminent musicians who came to Baden, including the Florentine Quartet, Rubinstein, Jaëll, Ernst, Sivori, Joachim, Stockhausen, Brahms, Levi, and many others. We had music to our hearts' content, and friends were invited to share our enjoyment. Many notable people were among them. Ludwig Bamberger, the well-known member of the Reichstag in Bismarck's time, who often stayed in Baden with his charming wife. His tall, spare, stooping figure, his plain features and sickly complexion, had been familiar to us on the Promenade. When we came to know him, we found him a man of the world, with perfect manners, eminent social gifts, and quick understanding of even the small everyday interests of others. With genuine affability he did not disdain to give young and inexperienced people the benefit of his ripe knowledge. When later on, as a widower, he retired to Interlaken, Marie and I met him again and became his near neighbours. He helped us in many ways, particularly when we were building our house there in 1897 after my mother's death. Unfortunately, we only enjoyed a single summer of this agreeable intercourse, for he died in the following year.

Then there was Fanny Lewald,[1] of whom I remember no more, I am sorry to say, than that her eyes, though keenly observant and intelligent, were like black pins on a pincushion ; that her husband, Adolf Stahr, used to kiss her hands frequently ; and that she asked my mother once how she could possibly manage to get on without a maid.

Anselm Feuerbach, the artist, came to our house several times, and brought his mother, Henriette Feuerbach, of whom I was childish enough to be frightened because I saw in her a resemblance to my former tormentor, Fräulein Hillebrand. Feuerbach was at that time struggling hard for recognition as an artist. His art had raised a fierce controversy ; a small, devoted group of admirers was pitched against an indifferent or hostile majority. Our friends belonged to the camp of his admirers, and were daily discussing the problems of art which his methods had raised, so we were anxious to make his personal acquaintance. He came, was interesting to look at with his fiery blue eyes and mop of wavy black hair, but his taciturnity thwarted all our attempts at nearer approach.

One day, when I happened to be in my mother's room, Mme. Viardot-Garcia was announced. I had seen her a few times when I was a child, but now realised her for the first time. A tall, elegant woman, quietly but very stylishly dressed, came into the room, ran up to my mother, hugged her and kissed her on both cheeks—that is to say, she put her cheek to my mother's and kissed the air, crying, ' Mein Klärchen ! mein Klärchen ! ' I had never seen this performance before, and looked on with much curiosity. I noticed that her face was oval, her eyes dark and rather Chinese and short-sighted, her nose straight and well shaped, with unusually large nostrils. A sensitive mouth, which she used to purse up, showed dimples in both cheeks when she talked or smiled. Short curls escaped from her bonnet, and large gold rings were suspended from her ears. She was not beautiful, I even

[1] Novelist and biographer.

PAULINE VIARDOT-GARCIA

thought her features plain, but they possessed an exotic and fascinating charm which held the eyes riveted upon them. Her manner was that of a great lady, self-assured, vivacious, and energetic in every movement; her conversation was sparkling and original. Her whole personality expressed joy of life, of activity and movement.

My mother introduced me. Mme. Viardot put her head back and a little on one side to take my measure for a moment; her slit eyes narrowed and her wide nostrils dilated still farther. Then she said a few kind words and shook hands with me. The two friends sat down; their pleasure at seeing each other again was evident. How different they were! My mother with her thoroughly German simplicity, and the other with her exotic look. Yet a sincere friendship had united them since they were girls; it survived long years of separation, and even the Franco-German War.

Mons. Viardot had been exiled during Napoleon the Third's reign, and settled with his family in Baden in 1862. They lived in a pretty chalet on the Fremersberger Road, which soon became the centre of social intercourse. Two charming and clever daughters, Klaudia and Marianne, graced the house. A large number of pupils of all nationalities followed in Mme. Viardot's train, and before long a cheerful musical activity developed in which the whole of Baden took an interest. The eldest daughter, Louise, a very talented musician, I hardly knew; she had just become engaged to be married, for I remember my mother telling us that Mme. Viardot had called to tell her of the engagement. She had said that the young people had not known each other long, but that they were well suited to each other, and the circumstances as favourable as possible. When my mother had earnestly inquired, 'But are they really in love with each other?' Mme. Viardot had laughingly embraced her and said, 'Oh, you dear German Klärchen!'

Iwan Turgeniev, the friend of the Viardot family, had built a chalet opposite to theirs ; he lived in it for many years, a voluntary exile. He was then not yet fifty, but snow-white hair framed his noble, spiritualised features, which, like his physique, were of a distinctly Slav type. I frequently met him in the course of the summer, as I soon became friendly with the Viardot girls, and I had the opportunity of seeing him in the intimate family circle, but I cannot remember anything he said. Although I am sorry for this now, at the time I was content merely to look at him. A wonderful serenity seemed the keynote of his being, and found expression in the benevolent gaze of his pale-blue eyes.

The construction of a charming little theatre in the garden of Mme. Viardot's villa was a great event. She probably intended that her pupils should gain their first operatic experiences there, or her own vivacious nature needed an outlet. Whatever the motive, the audiences thoroughly enjoyed themselves. Mme. Viardot herself wrote the music of several operettas to words by Turgeniev ; the parts were specially adapted to the capabilities of the performers. I remember several charming duets for her daughters' small, sympathetic voices, and a comic air for Paul, the only son, then eight years old, which he sang with such verve and virtuosity that the audience was electrified. Turgeniev himself played the title part in the operetta ' L'Ogre ' ; the pupils took the solo parts or sang in the choruses ; Mme. Viardot conducted the performances from the piano which was placed on one side of the stage. The house was always packed ; it was considered one of the greatest distinctions to be given an invitation to one of these performances. The King and Queen of Prussia with their Court were often present. The artists great and small reaped enthusiastic applause, but I do not think there was a more appreciative spectator than my mother. She followed the performances with heartfelt enjoyment, and spoke for days afterwards of her friend's genius, which embraced such a wide field. Different as they were from my mother's, the gifts of this remarkable woman were indeed amazingly many-sided. As an operatic singer she stood at the head of her profession ; she was a pianist of no mean attainments, for she had been a pupil of Liszt as a girl of sixteen, before she began to study for the stage ; she improvised, composed, spoke six languages fluently, had a distinct talent for drawing, and a practical gift for making a success of everything she undertook. In the 'sixties she still sometimes sang at concerts in Baden-Baden. Her voice did not strike me as beautiful so much as powerful ; it was a little hard. But her technique was brilliant and her coloratura perfect. The temperament of her race made every performance of hers an artistic experience to the hearer. I could not get her ' J'ai perdu mon Eurydice ' out of my mind for months.

She once sang a duet with a tenor, when her part ended with a shake. She held on and on ; the audience was breathless ; her partner glanced at her in amazement, then he offered her a chair. She smiled and continued her shake. He drew out his watch and held it towards her. When at last she ended with a perfect appogiatura, the audience broke into thunderous applause. An encore was insisted upon ; she sat down at the piano and sang a Chopin mazurka to French words. Turning sideways to her audience, she gave a performance such as I have never seen or heard since. She sang, spoke, acted, smiled so that each individual felt she was singing, speaking, smiling for him alone. Not a muscle in her face remained inactive ; vitality, fire, charm animated every feature. Had it been done for mere effect by any one not a genius, one would have thought it grotesque, but no one could ever have felt this about Pauline Viardot. She studied effects in minutest detail ; but is not that the highest art which, after having given the artist sleepless nights and many hours of strenuous work, appears perfectly simple and spontaneous ? Pauline Viardot's art was like this. She gave herself, expressed her own personality to perfection. From head to foot she was the Southerner ; German culture had influenced her without taking away from her originality.

And now that I have tried in many words to describe her, I read again her letter of June 11, 1892, in the third volume of Litzmann's *Klara Schumann*, and I ask myself if anything that I can say could ever give approximately as vivid a picture of her as does this single letter ? It is just like her and like my own recollection of her.

Two of our most intimate friends were Herr and Frau Rosenhain. We are glad to remember the kindly couple, their beaming faces and little curly fringes. Julie christened them ' the Lilliputians,' but in the vernacular they were known as ' the Hebrews from the Falkensteg,' where at the foot of the hill Merkur they had their charming summer residence, while they spent the winter in Paris. They could be seen every afternoon driving up and down the Lichtenthal Avenue—that is to say, the victoria was to be seen ; closer observation revealed the little couple tucked away in the corners. Their beautiful Newfoundland dog had made himself their forerunner ; he jumped at the horses in turn, running backwards all the time and barking loudly. This seemed to be a soothing lullaby to the occupants of the carriage, for I have often seen them asleep during the performance. But one day the wretched quadruped did it once too often ; his fate overtook him and he was killed.

My mother had a great regard for Herr Rosenhain because he had remained her faithful friend in spite of my father's devastating criticism of his later works. There was no bitterness in him who had met with many disappointments after starting his career as a promising pianist. To my mother he would sometimes open his heart when one after another his expectations of success failed ; other people always found him serene and good-humoured. His long sojourn in Paris had given his wit and conversational powers a fine polish. The little couple were very fond of each other, although they were for ever squabbling, and one was in despair when the other was ill. I used to be frequently the object of his wit, and when he began, ' Now, my charming antagonist,' I knew that I was in for a duel in which I had to summon all my powers of repartee to parry his thrusts, much to my mother's and Frau Rosenhain's amusement.

One of the most vital personalities of our Baden circle was Hermann Levi. He was the son of a Rabbi, and out of love for his father he never consented to become a Christian. He was right. A conversion would have been a discord in an otherwise complete and harmonious character. Hermann Levi was the prototype of an aristocratic Jew ; both in appearance and in mental and moral qualities he could never have been taken for anything else. His features had classic beauty and Oriental colouring ; his forehead was high and bold, his eyes, of indefinable colour, unusually keen, intelligent, and luminous. Unfortunately, this magnificent head was not matched by his body, which was small. He was for ever on the move. A man of thirty at that time, he had been conductor at the Karlsruhe Opera House for several years. The singers and actors of Karlsruhe were engaged to give a certain number of performances in Baden-Baden. These were great days for us. It was a joy to go to a theatre with my mother, for she gave herself up completely to the impressions of the play. We heard perfect performances of ' Figaro,' ' Barbiere,' ' The Magic Flute,' the ' Midsummer Night's Dream,' and other operas in the pretty little theatre. Levi was an eminent conductor, who got the utmost out of the forces at his disposal. He was very popular with singers and orchestra ; and though he always carried the day when there were differences of opinion, he retained their full devotion. Finally—and this was probably the secret of his success—he imparted to all the performers a great deal of the fire of his enthusiasm, which was his salient feature. It was inspiring to see this little man direct from his throne all the forces under his command. Perfect mastery of all his resources gave every line of his body perfect repose. His joy in his work and ever fresh enthusiasm added a delightful charm to all the performances under his conductorship. It was perhaps not an integral part of these that he often turned round to my mother, who was sitting behind him in the stalls, when he came to his favourite passages ; yet it was part of himself. In all that he did he needed ready sympathy and response, and he could always be sure of that from my mother. It was the greatest inspiration to Levi ; indeed, her generous appreciation of their success was their best reward to many musicians. Through our acquaintance with Levi social intercourse in our house became most animated, as the theatrical element also was drawn into our circle. Singers and actors came and went, foremost among them the manager of the Grand-ducal Theatres, Eduard Devrient, and Levi himself, whose visits were not only a momentary but a lasting stimulus to every one. Of course, he came chiefly on our mother's account, but he did not grudge us children a cheerful hour of his company. He had rarely been long in the house before we heard his knock and

(Scherzo from *Midsummer Night's Dream*.)

at the door of our room. Then his head would be peeping round the door with his beautiful and—I can find no other expression—'poking' eyes ; he would take everything in at a glance. He usually went to the piano at once and played what came into his head, sense and nonsense. I remember the 'Blue Danube' in different keys in each hand, excruciating but very jolly; then he would look at us in turn to see how we took it.

He often asked us to play duets with him, but with the exception of Elise none of us had the courage. General as Levi's culture was, music was so ingrained in him that he could never detach himself from it, while my mother, as well as Brahms and Joachim, quite happily relaxed from it for hours together. There was a good deal of the boy in Levi, and his laughter, which was more like bleating, was most infectious; it set his whole body and every muscle of his face quivering. One day he was in our room when the bell rang. 'That's Brahms,' he cried; 'hide me, quick!' He was hardly inside my mother's large travelling-trunk, which happened to be standing in the room, and we had shut the lid, when there was a knock at the door and Brahms came in. 'Where is he?' 'Who?' 'Well, he, Levi, isn't he here?' 'No, Levi isn't here.' 'Oh, I beg pardon, I must have made a mistake,' Brahms said, rather embarrassed, and retired towards the door, when

(Ninth Symphony.)

issued from the box, and the bird escaped from his cage. Another time he brought his 'Schufterle' (Scamp), a large St. Bernard dog. It was on some festive occasion, and we were drinking champagne, beloved by all the Schumanns. Levi, who was in great spirits, held his glass towards the dog, thinking no doubt that he would turn away in disgust. But not a bit of it ! ' Scamp ' knew better. He lapped his fizz like a toper, and in spite of my mother's shocked ' Oh, Levi, Levi ! ' he let him empty the glass. Before many minutes were gone, the creature turned round and round, performed the most amazing antics, and in the end became so mad that we predicted his early death. But faster than human beings on these occasions he recovered ; and if it was his first, it was probably not his last experience of champagne.

Levi, Allgeyer, and Brahms were inseparable companions for the time being, both in Karlsruhe and in Baden. A curiously contrasting team ! Levi the Oriental, vivacious, restless ; Brahms as German, and specifically North German, as he could be, warm-hearted, but usually hiding his deeply passionate nature under an appearance of ruggedness. And between these two thoroughbreds the tall, bony Suabian with his kind brown eyes and his indescribably slow movements and talk. To his two friends he was an object of anxious care, for in spite of great accomplishments he never made a success of anything. It was touching to hear the other two making plans and trying again and again to find the right place for him.

Brahms and Allgeyer had already been friends in Düsseldorf, and met again in Baden, where Levi made the third in their alliance. His eminent musical achievements led naturally to an acquaintance with Brahms, for whose compositions he had conceived an enthusiastic admiration. This gave an element of warmth to their relations. When in later years this enthusiasm cooled, their friendship instantly fell to the ground. The change of front in Levi towards his former friend had been sudden and ruthless. Brahms told us that he had arrived in Munich with his box full of new compositions, and Levi had not even asked him if he had brought anything to show him. Probably the purely human

HERMANN LEVI

points, of contact between them had never existed, and without these no friendship can be lasting.

An example, though slight in itself, will sufficiently characterise the difference in their outlook upon human relations. It has remained so vividly in my memory that I will try to tell it as much as possible in Brahms's own words.

'You remember,' he said, 'that Levi had a man and wife living with him as servants. The man was a decent fellow, and valeted him to his satisfaction. One day Levi noticed that cigars were missing from a box which he had left open on his table. He put a piece of paper on top of the cigars with the words, " Is the theft of cigars no theft ? " Next day the man came to him and said, " I confess to stealing the cigars, and beg to give warning." Do you see,' said Brahms with passionate anger in his steel-blue eyes, ' what a terrible wrong Levi has done to this man ? If you don't want to share your cigars with your valet, lock them up, but don't lead him into temptation and then ruin him.'

Few of Brahms's words have made a deeper impression on me, not only on account of the feeling they expressed, but because they were so characteristic of the man. He was of the people, and it was infinitely to his credit that he had never lost touch with them. He had known what temptation meant. He had a warm heart for the needy, and eased their burdens where he could do so without ostentation. During the time of his conductorship in Vienna he worked unremittingly to improve conditions for the members of his orchestra, and what I remember him to have said on this point shows how much he had it at heart.

Our feelings towards these three intimates were mixed. Levi was always welcome, but we thought Allgeyer such a bore that we could not do with him at all. Levi tried to convert us ; his remonstrance, ' Fräulein Marie, two hours alone in Allgeyer's company would show you what kind of a man he is,' gave rise to much teasing of her to whom they were addressed.

Brahms we took for granted. There he was, always had been, and always would be ; he was one of us. The schoolgirl in me resented his neglect of appearances ; his coloured shirts without collars, his little alpaca coats, and the trousers which were always too short, were a thorn in my flesh. But the elasticity of his gait, with the weight thrown on the heels, pleased me when I saw him coming towards the house, hat in hand. He cared nothing for polite manners, but as he was at times painfully conscious of his awkwardness, he was rather shy as a young man and tried to hide this shyness under a certain bluntness. His cover was always laid for him, and he came and went as he liked, in good or bad mood, bringing now good, now bad hours. Like Levi, he would frequently come to our room and play to us : Schubert dances or his own Valses, op. 39, and wonderful, melancholy Hungarian melodies for which I have looked in vain among his published works ; perhaps he never wrote them down.

The description of our Baden summer would be incomplete without mentioning the dear old friends of my mother, Fräulein Rosalie Leser and her companion and constant nurse, Fräulein Elise Jungé. The friendship dated from the Düsseldorf time, and had received its baptism during the days of deepest sorrow. Fräulein Leser had shared in the happy times when my father was still with us. When his terrible fate overtook him she became a comfort and help to my mother in devoted sympathy and unfailing encouragement. She was blind— not from birth but from her ninth year, so that she knew what she had lost ; she also suffered a great deal of pain in her eyes. But she never complained ; with wonderful strength of mind she had taken her life in her hands and moulded it entirely to the welfare of others. Her room became a centre for her numerous relations, friends,

and acquaintances, who were certain at all times of
' Aunt Rosalchen's ' understanding sympathy for all
their great and small troubles. She had a keen intellect,
a warm heart, great tact, and absolute discretion. After
we had bought the Lichtenthal cottage she came to
Baden every summer, took rooms with the clergyman's
wife, our neighbour, and shared our lives. Fräulein
Jungé, her companion, was very fond of us children, and
we thoroughly appreciated her kindness and her touchingly childlike nature. Every morning, directly after
breakfast, they used to slip through the hedge into our
garden to sit with our mother ; Fräulein Leser doing
crochet-work or, a favourite occupation of hers, slicing
beans for the whole large party. Our mother talked all
her concerns over with her, not only because she liked
to do so, but with a desire to brighten the darkness of
her blind friend's life. However pressing her professional duties might be, Fräulein Leser was never allowed
to go short ; she received her letters quite regularly, so
that she was kept in touch with our lives. Twice a year
my mother went to Düsseldorf to see her, usually stayed
with her, played to her, and even found time to take
her out for walks, when a ray of supreme happiness
would light up the blind face.

As in the days of our childhood, I too would constantly
slip through the gap in the hedge to see my friend
Elisabeth. She had grown into a lovely girl. Sweetly
and frankly her blue eyes looked out upon the world,
and again thoughtfully and seriously. I have always
thought that Goethe's Friederike von Sesenheim must
have been like that. Elisabeth's father had been a
minister of the Lutheran Church, but had retired from
office by the time when we made their acquaintance.
His second wife, Elisabeth's mother, a tall, handsome
woman with noble features animated by good sense and
kindness, was the sister of a Roman Catholic priest, and
herself a devout Roman Catholic. After her father's

death, not only Elisabeth and her younger brother and sister, but also their elder stepbrother, became Roman Catholics. For Elisabeth this was a time of happy excitement, and my scepticism concerning her resolution could not shake her.

What happy hours we spent in the arbour of the neighbouring garden or in their small old-fashioned drawing-room, where a portrait of Jung-Stilling (Goethe's friend) hung on the wall ! He had been Elisabeth's grandfather. She married, and died young after having borne two sons. I have kept the memory of this friend fresh in my heart, and cannot picture the Baden summer without her dear and bright presence.

Truly, it was a summer glowing with sun, life, and love. I see everything before me as though it had been yesterday. Our own little cottage, large enough to give each of us a separate room ; the dormer windows that looked out upon the lovely surroundings ; the large wardrobe room where innumerable pretty summer dresses, freshly washed and starched, were kept. My three charming sisters, all dressed alike in white and blue. (This was the taste of Princess Anna of Hesse, which she gratified herself in princely fashion.) I myself, in spite of my seventeen years still very much of a schoolgirl, feeling a little out of place ; at times checked, but usually much spoilt. My beloved Felix home for the holidays, and Ferdinand for Julie's wedding. What sunny excursions we had to the Old Castle, the Yburg, Ebersteinschloss, and Gernsbach, usually in company of our friends ; drives back in the moonlight, indescribable sensations at issuing from the dark woods into moonlit openings ! What noble interests I was privileged to share ; and, above all, what waves of wonderful music daily flowed for us !

With poignant clearness some moments stand out specially, such as when two or three of us were going into the little town and our beloved mother would see

us off and kiss us as though we were taking leave for
a long separation. ' Children, keep your backs straight,'
used to be her last words, while we turned round once
more to her who stood on the steps looking after us with
indescribable tenderness. Remembrance of moments
like these makes me feel as if my heart would break
with longing.

And yet, clouds were gathering about us once more
even in this sunniest of summers. Ludwig, though still
with us, was driven farther and farther apart from us by
his melancholia, and in August he had to be put under
a doctor's care. No wonder that my mother, who moreover dreaded the separation from Julie, was often deeply
depressed. The buoyancy of our youth kept joy and
cheerfulness uppermost in spite of everything.

Julie's *fiancé*, to whom we soon became devoted,
arrived on September 14, and the wedding took place
in the chapel of the Lichtenthal Convent on the 22nd.
Then we took leave of her, and in the later part of the
day the house was wrapped in deep silence. Marie and
I were sitting sadly in the dining-room when the bell
rang, and we heard Brahms go to our mother's room.
Soon afterwards deeply stirring and solemn music
reached our ears. We listened. Brahms went away,
and our mother came to us in a state of great emotion.
Brahms had played her his Rhapsody for an alto voice
(op. 53) for the first time.

That is my last recollection of the summer of 1869.
Our boxes were packed, the cottage, which was never
again to unite us all under its roof, was locked up, the
key left with our kind neighbour, and we were scattered
once more in all directions. My mother started on her
winter concert tour, and I was sent to Berlin as a student
at the College of Music, which had just been opened.

THINGS GAY AND GRAVE
(1869-1871)

ONCE more I found myself in strange surroundings, but not wholly among strangers, for Joseph Joachim, the Director of the College, had long been our most faithful friend, and when, as one of the pupils, I now came into a new relationship with him, I felt how close were the ties that bound us together. He was dignified but kind, and could often let himself go in friendly and childlike gaiety. There was so much sincerity in his look, so much real kindness in his words, that one could not help being fond of him.

Ernst Rudorff was my piano teacher. He had been a pupil of my mother's, when in spite of his youth he became her friend. He too was therefore no stranger to me. At that time I saw in him merely a young man with a rather awkward manner, reddish hair and blue eyes, who taught us very conscientiously and made us feel that our progress was of importance to him. Now I know that he was one of those artists who deserve remembrance for their strong individuality and in grateful acknowledgment of what they achieved.

He has left no great works to hand down his fame to posterity, but Schiller's words, ' He who appealed to the best of his time has lived for all times,' may well be said of Ernst Rudorff. Truly, they were the best of his time whom he numbered among his friends and whose ideals he shared. He brought great moral qualities and enthusiasm to the task of teaching the younger generation to realise the best in art and understand the works of the great masters. He had to fight for his ideals. A fiery temperament, a natural desire to share his knowledge, a gift for understanding others and making himself understood, a young, cheerful, and—last, not least—kind heart : these were his weapons. He never yielded ground an inch where the best, truest, and greatest in art was concerned.

At first we were only three pupils, and the lessons proceeded in a quiet and sedate way. One day, however, when I came into the classroom, Professor Rudorff said to me, ' Let me introduce a new pupil to you, whose playing will interest you—Fräulein Natalie Janotha.' I saw a girl barely grown up, with short *cendré* curls, a white overall over her short dress, and a belt with an ample ' chatelaine.' A pair of sturdy legs in white stockings gave the finish to a babyish appearance. We shook hands and I sat down ; she squeezed herself on to the same chair, scrutinised me, and, as I seemed to pass muster, put her arm round my waist. Then she played to me, a charming bravura piece which ended with a musical-box. She imitated this with great skill, and altogether showed eminent talent for technique. The temperament of her Polish race was in every finger-tip.

Our lessons now became extremely animated, for Natalie was brimful of high spirits, and the young professor was often hard put to it to keep the necessary gravity. Respect due to elders was a word without meaning to Natalie. Once when he was correcting her hand and tried to give it the desired position by a slight turning of the wrist, the little person instantly withdrew it and slapped his. Another time, when he proposed that she should study Moscheles' Concerto in G minor, she dismissed it with ' Waste time ! ' We others could not help laughing on these occasions, and I thought it charming of Rudorff to join in the laugh, usually after a helpless look of appeal to me. One of her pranks ended so outrageously that he had to hide his laughter in his pocket-handkerchief. Another pupil was having her turn of the lesson, when we were of course supposed to keep absolute silence. Rudorff was standing behind his pupil, Natalie and I sitting behind him—Natalie on a music-stool, on which she was perpetually turning. ' Look,' she whispered, ' this time I shall make a complete turn,' started off and turned a somersault. When Rudorff looked round to see what the noise meant, Natalie and the music-stool were lying head downwards on the floor. Her long chain of garnets had been broken in the mêlée, and master and pupils crept about the room on all-fours to collect the beads from all the corners. It was a long time before gravity was restored in the sanctuary.

Rudorff's attempts to civilise the unruly Polish cub were very amusing. She could never be induced to say how old she was, and frequently contradicted herself on that point. Rudorff meant to settle it once and for all. He examined her strictly as to when and where she was born, christened, etc. He was not able to get to the bottom any more than we were, but he came to the conclusion, rightly or wrongly, that she was seventeen and not fifteen, and told her to own up to it when occasion arrived. She promised, and when soon afterwards a gentleman asked her in our presence, ' Quel âge avez-vous, mademoiselle ? ' she answered, ' Je crois que j'ai dix-sept ans.' ' Mais comment, mademoiselle, vous ne le savez donc pas ? ' Natalie looked at us in despair and stammered, ' Monsieur Rudorff l'a dit.'

Natalie and I soon made friends, and sometimes exercised the prerogative of such by falling out with each other. Once our quarrel was so serious that we were not on speaking terms during our lessons. This made our master most unhappy, and he took me aside and said desperately, ' But what is to happen if you two are never, never going to be friends again ? ' I went home in a half-obstinate, half-softened mood, and

JOSEPH JOACHIM
IN 1869

was walking along by the trees of the Tiergarten in bright moonlight, when suddenly Natalie came running after me and we fell into each other's arms. During the next lesson we were sharing a chair again, and our kindhearted professor's face beamed with satisfaction.

These little episodes were not, however, allowed to interfere with the seriousness of our studies. Indeed, Professor Rudorff made great demands on us, and we worked hard. Natalie made brilliant progress ; mine was hampered as before by my insufficient technique. Rudorff took great pains with it, but continual writing in Rödelheim, sometimes for whole days, and later on a great deal of croquet, for which I used my left hand, had probably spoilt my hands for piano-playing.

Joachim often listened to our lessons. One day this great artist came with his violin under his arm, saying that Professor Rudorff was ill and he would make up for the loss of our lessons by playing a sonata with each of us. He made me play the small Mozart one in E minor at sight, and had kind words of praise for my reading it like a musician. I often listened to the orchestral practices which he conducted, and he would remind me of my mother in his ceaseless endeavour to get the greatest possible perfection out of the young students, rehearsing special difficulties over and over until he was satisfied with the result.

I was a boarder in a Berlin family. On Sundays I usually met my brothers. In the forenoons, which are the proper time for formal calls, Ferdinand and I went the round of a large number of friends, and we received many invitations. We usually met at some appointed street corner, and when we had greeted each other gladly and affectionately he would scrutinise my appearance carefully, especially when I was wearing a new frock. ' Are you sure you are dressed quietly enough ? ' he would anxiously ask before he took me to the Café Kranzler in Unter den Linden, and while

I ate éclairs he instructed me how to behave on the forthcoming visits. 'We must never stay longer than seven minutes, and it is for you as the lady to get up to go.'

The three of us had standing invitations to Sunday dinners alternately at the Adolf Schwabes' and the Eckerts' (Herr Eckert was conductor at the Royal Opera House), who received us as though we were their own children. I gratefully remember the kindness with which both these families made up to us for the want of a home. Both hostesses, each in her own way, showed me great affection.

Ferdinand had grown into a handsome young man ; with his pleasant manners he made himself liked everywhere. Felix, a youth of fifteen, was still a little shy and dreamy, but his thoughtful eyes were nevertheless observant, and he would often make remarks on the way home which betrayed unusual insight. In the afternoons we used to go to Ferdinand's rooms, where we played duets, his favourite pastime, supped simply together, and parted as late as possible. We often went to the Joachim Quartet evenings and many other concerts together ; heard Tausig, whose playing left us cold. But Rubinstein swept us altogether off our feet. He gave a number of concerts in the course of the winter, for which he had instructed his agent to send us three Schumann tickets. Our seats were on the platform close to the piano, so that we could follow each passionate mood on his mobile face, see every movement of his large hands with their unusually blunt finger-tips, and even the drops of blood on the keys. Berlin lost its head entirely, and we three were no exception. I was in such a state of enthusiasm that I could think of nothing day and night but Rubinstein. Natalie did not have to use much persuasion when she proposed that I should accompany her on a visit to him. Rubinstein had taken an interest in her studies from the first, given her advice, and was ready to give her an interview. I

myself as a child had seen him in Baden. We set out
cheerfully on our adventure one day after our lesson.
If my visit surprised him, Rubinstein did not show it ;
his affability was altogether charming. He asked how
Mamma and Marie were, how Natalie was getting on,
and so forth, and dismissed us after half an hour. Natalie,
claiming the prerogative of Polish custom, kissed his
hands, even his sleeves. I looked on, half embarrassed,
half envious. But I fully appreciated the dignified
manner in which this distinguished artist and man of the
world knew how to deal with his youthful admirers.

I returned to the Pension flushed with happy excitement. ' Just think, I have met Rubinstein ! ' ' Rubinstein ? Where ? ' ' At his hotel ! ' ' Incredible ! shock-
ing ! ' descended like a cold douche upon me. A worse
shower-bath followed when I was told that they could
not keep a young girl who was capable of doing such a
thing ; that my mother must be told ; and so on and so
forth. I said that I should tell her myself as a matter
of course. These good people were quite justified, but
oh ! how they damped my spirits ! I gave Mamma
an account of the whole adventure at once, and she did
not reproach me with one word. She knew what enthusiasm such as this meant. And I myself am glad to this
day that I went to see Rubinstein—even in his hotel in
Unter den Linden !

I returned to the Baden cottage in the following spring.
We were looking forward to a happy summer, when the
declaration of war came upon us like a bolt from the
blue. The excitement was indescribable. Apart from
the appalling fact itself, our living so near the frontier
was sufficient reason for filling us with apprehension.
Visitors were soon scattered in all directions, and the
town looked desolate. Our mother was greatly per-
turbed ; her imagination dwelt on the horrors of an
invasion, and she was inconsolable at the thought that
the Maroccan soldiers might destroy her Apollo and

Venus. ' Herr Rosenhain, what shall we do if there is a French invasion ? ' she asked.

' Have no fear, Frau Schumann ; the French are a charming people, they will do no harm.'

' Pauline, what shall we do if there is a French invasion ? '

' The first thing we have to do is to take our daughters to a place of safety,' was Mme. Viardot's answer.

After the declaration of war Mons. Viardot had at once left for France. Mme. Viardot and her children remained in Baden. They and the other French inhabitants could do so in perfect safety. Nothing was known at that time of concentration camps, internment, or confiscation of enemy property. It is not our country which can boast of having invented these measures, not German brains that thought of anything so monstrous. Mme. Viardot and her daughters remained where they were, and helped in the work for wounded soldiers. Her skill in designing and cutting out garments was much admired. News of our victories soon arrived, following closely upon each other. Mme. Viardot's self-possession was admirable. But when the final news of the surrender of Sedan and Napoleon's captivity found its way into our workrooms, she got up and put down her scissors, saying, ' Venez, mes enfants,' and went out with her daughters. A few days later they left for Paris, never to return to Baden. Her house and theatre, which had witnessed so many hours of social and artistic enjoyment, remained shut for years ; the poet-friend's cottage opposite theirs was also left deserted. Whenever we passed we thought sadly of the beloved and admired friends who had left us for ever. The eye of the law watched over these homes as vigilantly as over those of our own citizens. The owners would have found everything as they left it, had they returned. Who will blame them that they did not find it in their hearts to do so ?

Our mother, too, had at first thought of leaving Baden,

but our friends persuaded her to stay, and the good news from the front soon reassured us. We were witnesses of part of the fighting when we went up to the Old Castle, the Yburg, or Windeck. Our eyes roamed the wide expanse of the Rhine Valley, and the first cannonades made our hearts quail. On clear days we could see the spire of Strasbourg Cathedral, little thinking that the time was near when the betrayal of 1681 would be avenged and Strasbourg returned to our Fatherland. The siege began at the end of August. Our cottage trembled with the reverberation of the heavy guns, and Mamma wept bitter tears for the fate of those against whom they were directed. On September 27 the fortress surrendered ; two days later Levi persuaded us to let him take us over to see a German Strasbourg. The day was gloriously fine, an autumn day with summer's sun and heat ; our hearts beat high. Thousands went on the same errand. We were obliged to leave the train at Kehl ; the railway bridge had been destroyed, and a pontoon bridge connected the banks of the Rhine. First we visited the fortifications, where our guns had worked fearful destruction ; exploded and unexploded shells were lying about, and the sentries warned us to be careful. We went to the Cathedral, which so far as I remember was untouched. The town had a melancholy look ; the few inhabitants who showed themselves went about looking dejected and frightened. We had dinner at a small inn, and our excitement ran so high that when Levi soon afterwards felt unwell we feared that he had been poisoned. Fortunately, he soon recovered. We took the last train back. The crowd was enormous. The people climbed on to the roofs of the carriages, were ordered off, climbed on again, so that the officials were obliged to give the signal for the departure of the train. And with all these singing, trampling, shouting revellers overhead we travelled homewards.

Although our parents both came of pure Saxon stock and we children were legally Saxons, we felt we were

Germans first and foremost, and looked upon the war from this standpoint. But I found with surprise that not every one felt like this in the Duchy of Baden. When Marie and I one day went into the town to ask for news and passed our neighbour's cottage, Elisabeth looked out of the window and cried cheerfully, ' Have you heard ? The Prussians have had one in the eye at Bar-le-Duc ! ' Some forty years later her son died a hero's death for his country. *He* no longer knew of any difference between German and German.

In spite of my eighteen years I had never read a newspaper except the local Baden one, which was quite good. My mother, although interested in politics so far as they concerned Germany, had positively not the time to read newspapers. But now Marie and I felt the need of reliable news from France, and started to take in the *Augsburger Allgemeine Zeitung*. We had been certain of the successful ending of the war since the victory of Sedan, and this made us indescribably happy. Even as a child I had often realised with resentment that the Germans were treated with contempt in their own country by their cosmopolitan visitors in Baden-Baden, or at best with a pitying condescension. Yet we Germans knew what we were worth, and that we ought to take our place with the great nations. We did not yet see the full import of our great victory—the years that followed made it clearer to us ; but we knew that these were great times, and that the outcome for our Fatherland would be its rightful place, of which it had been deprived for centuries.

In the course of this summer our harmless little River Oos, whose gentle murmurs accompanied our work by day and our dreams at night, played us a nasty trick. A still smaller and apparently more harmless sister, whose existence we had hardly noticed, aided and abetted her. This came down from the hill Merkur, disappeared below the village street opposite our house, and joined the elder sister by a subterranean channel. We had had several

FRAU SCHUMANN'S COTTAGE IN BADEN-BADEN

After a small oil-painting which Brahms had ordered to be made and presented to the Schumann family

days of heavy rain, and were watching the rising of the Oos with surprise but without apprehension. In the early hours of one morning, however, Marie was awakened by the noise of rushing waters, which seemed to come from the basement. She jumped out of bed and down the stairs, and when she had reached the head of the kitchen stairs she saw a swirling flood filling the kitchen. She looked at it horror-struck, then hastily roused us, saying that the walls could not possibly stand the force of the waters. I dressed and ran down to see the devastation. The whole village was astir. Men stood with long poles on the bridge, which was already partly flooded, and pushed logs and other floating objects under the arches to prevent its destruction. I ran back upstairs, and found my mother in hat and mantilla on the landing, with three large volumes bound in Russia leather under her arm ; they were a collected edition of my father's works which a Russian publisher who was not restricted by copyrights had recently sent her. She has often been teased about this choice.

Fortunately, we were able to avert a catastrophe to our cottage. There happened to be among the men on the bridge a stonemason who had built our basement, and he offered his help. He went into the water with lighterman's boots, looked for and found in the cellar adjoining the kitchen a stone trap. This he lifted, and the water gradually ran off into the Oos, which was subsiding. Evidently floods had been reckoned with when the house was built.

' How happy I am that the children are so cheerful ! ' was an entry in my mother's diary. Yes, cheerful we were notwithstanding Ludwig's mental state, which was now declared incurable and threw a shadow over our lives, and in spite of war. We were young, life was worth living, we had a happy home. Indeed, I felt more and more at home, drew closer every day to Marie. But an unconquerable feeling of shyness still separated me from my mother; I never went to her of my own accord. Then one day—I cannot tell how or why it happened, but an irresistible impulse drew me towards her. It came over me like a revelation that this regal woman was my own mother, that she belonged to me, and I and all we children were the dearest beings on earth to her. I approached her from behind, gently put my arms round her neck and said softly, 'My little Mother!' The spell was broken, every trace of shyness gone; this moment was the beginning of a friendship which deepened more and more with the years and gave my life its true value and consecration.

My mother again gave me music lessons twice a week. I studied the more difficult sonatas by Beethoven, and my father's Phantasiestücke, op. 12, and the Novelettes. In the autumn I returned to Berlin for several months. Life at the College of Music went on as usual. We two friends again sat on the same chair, our professor was charming, and we worked enthusiastically. Natalie was studying Mendelssohn's G minor Concerto; I, Beethoven's in C minor.

Our brother Ferdinand had been conscripted and was in France, but as he had not yet been trained as a soldier he was not sent to the front. We were therefore in no great anxiety on his account, and did not guess that exposure and over-exertion during his training were to lay the foundation of the rheumatic trouble which afflicted him for many years, and of which he eventually died.

In November my mother and Marie came to Berlin and stayed for several weeks. Natalie played to my mother, who promised to take her as a pupil during the summer, while Rudorff should teach her during the winter months.

My mother departed for Breslau on the 2nd of January, when I went through a terrible experience. I had spent the previous evening with her at her hotel, and she had scolded me for some reason. I do not remember the cause of her displeasure, but I know that I took it badly, flung out of her room and went home. When I awoke quite early the next morning, my first thought was, ' Mamma is leaving in an hour's time, and she is annoyed with me ! ' I was in despair ; dressed, and ran out of the house. It was still dark and the cold was intense. Mamma's diary says, ' The coldest journey I have ever had.' The omnibuses had not yet started running, and I hurried on in the direction where I knew the station to be, but I had never been there before. After three-quarters of an hour's run I arrived, rushed up to the platform—thank God ! the train had not yet started. But all the doors were closed and not a guard was to be seen. They had probably already clambered into their little hutches on the top of the carriages. I jumped on to the footboard of the first carriage and tried to look in, but the closed window was covered with thick ice. I went from carriage to carriage—the same stern, impenetrable barrier everywhere ! Behind one of those windows was my beloved mother, ignorant of my grief. A shrill whistle—and the train departed. I have seen it standing there and departing a thousand times over, and can still feel the agony of that moment. These cold, blind windows seemed to stand for the anger of God. I wrote to my mother the same day ; she returned after two days, and all was well.

At the end of January we went to England, where I spent three glorious months. We were the guests of Mr. and Miss Burnand, brother and sister, in Hyde Park Gate, who received us with real affection in their refined, comfortable home—luxurious, as it would have been called by German standards. But in England these comforts did not mean a snobbish display of wealth, but were the usual surroundings of the upper classes. Their habits, and still more those of their servants, each of whom did only a certain strictly circumscribed amount of work, resembled each other in all the homes.

Nothing seemed to give Mr. Burnand greater pleasure than to show Marie and me the sights of London. Carriages and servants were always at our disposal ; we were taken in the greatest comfort and without fatigue to see the Tower, the Docks, the Mint, the General Post Office, the British Museum, exhibitions of pictures of Old Masters, the Boat Race, and many other interesting things. We went to every theatre, saw Sheridan played to great perfection, but there was not a single theatre where a Shakespeare play could be seen.

We often drove in the Park in the afternoons to catch a glimpse of the lovely Princess of Wales. The footman on the box had been instructed to give the signal when she was in sight, and each time our carriage attracted the great lady's eyes our friends beamed. At first I thought it my duty to bow, and she acknowledged this very kindly, but Miss Burnand told me it was not the custom to bow to members of the Royal Family, as the perpetual acknowledgments would make their drives irksome. I thought this custom, probably a tacit mutual understanding, very sensible. Mamma went for walks in the beautiful Park whenever she had a spare moment. She preferred the open spaces where one met the wind fully, and these were not difficult to find at this season. When we walked along the Serpentine and across the bridge, the wind would nearly blow us over ; it made these walks a misery to me, for I hated wind. I have since learnt to love it, and still love it.

English ways were not unfamiliar to me. Many of my fellow-pupils at Neu-Watzum had been English or Scottish, and I had liked their simple, natural manner and made friends with them. I had learnt to talk English fairly fluently, and it had amused them to teach me a little slang. When I came to know the English in their own country, I was chiefly struck with their natural self-assurance. From the railway employees with their calm civility and a touch of condescension towards foreigners, to the youngest housemaid in the Burnands' household, they all had a manner which one might well have envied them. Their way also of attaching little importance to small matters, and their ready helpfulness, were very sympathetic to me, and I liked a certain ingenuousness which sometimes, however, is the outcome of ignorance ; nevertheless, it is an agreeable feature. I was not yet old enough to form a definite opinion of the nation. As a guest and the child of my parents I was, moreover, in a privileged position. I owed the exceptional kindness shown to me to admiration for my parents ; on that point I was quite clear, but this did not at all diminish my enjoyment in my share of it. I made one friend of my own with whom I was in close touch until she died. She was the mother of three children ; frail, small, and delicate ; clever and full of varied interests. She spoke German fluently, was fond of everything German, and had a particular liking for Paul Heyse's books, so that she decided to translate his *Children of the World* into English. Although I did not share her taste for this book, I consented willingly to help her with the translation, and learnt a great deal through it and the correspondence with her.

The social life in London did not, on the whole, attract me very much ; I thought it monotonous and dull. I was often in the same room with interesting people, but either they were not introduced or were stand-offish. We met Mme. Viardot again ; she had fled from Paris with her daughters and was spending the winter in London. The daughters were much admired in London drawing-rooms for their charming singing of French duets to their mother's accompaniment.

An introduction which made me supremely happy was one to Jenny Lind. She was living in Wimbledon with her husband, Otto Goldschmidt, and her children, and Mamma and Marie were asked to spend a day with her. I had not been included in the invitation, and was miserable. Jenny Lind had held my small brothers and sisters on her knees ; I had been born too late, had never seen or heard her, but admiration for her had been instilled into me from babyhood. ' Mamma,' I begged, ' you simply must take me with you.' She smiled and did not say no. When she introduced me to our hostess, asking her forgiveness for bringing me, Jenny Lind looked at me sternly and said, ' So you have come unasked ? ' I was frightened for a moment, for I had heard a great deal about her forbidding manner, but I detected, or thought I detected, a gleam of humour in her eye, and courageously laid all my enthusiasm at her feet. We spent a delightful day. She continued to tease the uninvited guest, but I cannot have been altogether unsympathetic to the great artist, for did she not pick a sprig of scarlet blossom when I walked by her side in the garden that afternoon ? And did I not press that sprig and keep it to this day ?

For Mr. Goldschmidt the position as the husband of a celebrity was undoubtedly somewhat invidious, but the unfailing tact with which he met every situation could only be the outcome of genuine affection and admiration for his wife. My mother's wish that she should sing to us on this occasion remained unfulfilled, but I heard her sing some Mendelssohn and Schumann songs not long after at the house of one of our mutual friends. The charm of her singing was still undeniable, but her voice was gone, and so I cannot truly say that I have heard Jenny Lind sing. I have always considered it a real injustice of fate that I have never heard her or Mme. Schröder-Devrient at their best.

What I have said before about the social life in London does not apply in every case. There certainly were exceptions, and the Burnands were one of these. Brother and sister were temperamentally gay and possessed great social talents ; they made all their guests feel at their ease. During the time of our sojourn with them their numerous relations and friends dropped into the background, and only artists or persons who had a claim on my mother's attention were invited. At that time strict observance of the Sabbath was still general. But as artists, especially musicians, were busy every week-day in London or the provinces, the Burnands made an exception to the rule, and their Sunday evening parties were among the pleasantest of our London experiences. Dinner was early on these occasions, as my mother made it a rule to go to bed early on the day before a concert, and Mondays were concert days. The conversation at dinner was always most animated ; all the guests knew each other well and were interested in each other. The gentlemen told anecdotes of their concert tours in the provinces, and Mamma sometimes related amusing little incidents connected with one or other of the few pupils she consented to take during these months. One of them had played Schumann's ' Arabesque ' to her, but omitted the middle part. When Mamma in astonish-ment had asked her the reason why, she said, ' Papa doesn't like minor.' Once when Mamma was giving a lesson in the drawing-room, another pupil wished to speak to her. ' Mme. Schumann is engaged.' ' Then I will see Miss Schumann.' Miss Schumann also was engaged. Whereupon the young lady sent up a scrap of paper with the words, ' If the piece which is now being played in the drawing-room is by Schumann, I should like to learn it too.' But the piece happened to be by Mendelssohn.

As our hosts spoke no language but English, the general conversation was in English, and this was often a severe test for the gravity of the servants who waited at table. The phrasing and pronunciation of the guests often left a good deal to be desired. When the footman was asked by one of the artists who wished for more salmon, ' Gif me anozzer liddle fish, please,' he was able to keep his countenance pretty well ; but when Ernest Pauer, with

his comic face and in his best Viennese English, told a
story in which a nightcap played a prominent part, a
general breakdown followed. The footmen were clearing
the table for dessert ; the younger was holding firmly
pressed against his front the huge tray on which the
elder was placing the empty wine-glasses, when these
suddenly began to jingle. The little fellow was
shaking all over, and the facial contortions with which
he tried to hide his laughter were wonderful. The
moment came when he could bear it no longer : luckily
the sideboard was just behind him ; he dumped down
his tray and ran out of the room exploding. His elder
colleague followed, and even the butler collapsed — he
who had never been known to lose his dignity ran
after them.

Regular guests at these parties were Mr. Theophilus
Burnand, brother of our host, a charming old bachelor
who resembled Mr. Pickwick as he was then represented
on the stage. His amiable custom when he invited ladies
to dinner at his house was to put a gift of a dozen pairs
of gloves by their cover. Joseph Joachim and his
brother Henry with his charming young wife always
came; also the other members of the quartet, Piatti and
Strauss. These, with the artist Horsley and the sculptor
Westmacott, formed the nucleus ; the other guests, all
of whom would be selected to fit into the circle, were
not always the same. After dinner the quartet would
either rehearse their programme for the next evening,
or there was animated conversation. Once, as a surprise
for the Burnands, all the musicians joined in Haydn's
' Children's Symphony.' They stood round the piano ;
their parts were pinned on each other's backs. Joachim
looked longingly at each instrument, and would have
liked to play them all ; but as that could not be, he
finally decided for the cuckoo. They started—twenty-
four bars for the cuckoo to count, not an easy matter !
He came in wrongly each time, when a reproachful glance

from my mother, who presided at the piano with great earnestness, lighted on the naughty bird.

There are no people in the world more childlike than artists, especially musicians. Piatti was one of these ingenuous, easy-going natures—so easy-going, indeed, that my mother was in despair sometimes. When I heard a little story of his father, I understood from whom he had inherited his temperament. Alfred Piatti, being on a visit to his father, who was living in a small town in Northern Italy, begged him to pay him a visit in London some day. The father promised he would. 'You must write and tell me the time of your arrival,' said his son, ' so that I can meet you at Dover, or at least at the London terminus.' ' Oh, not at all necessary ; I shall pay you a surprise visit; I shall find you all right.' 'That is out of the question ; promise that you will write and let me know.' ' Oh, don't bother,' persisted the old man cheerfully, rejecting all good advice. One day he started for London, but forgot to take his son's address with him. He arrived safely, followed in the wake of a large number of people who alighted from various trains, and presently found himself on West-minster Bridge. Then he must have become a little doubtful, for he stopped a passer-by and uttered the one word, ' Piatti.' Marvellous to relate, the person thus addressed nodded, made him a sign to follow him, and took him to Covent Garden, where Piatti was playing in the orchestra. Imagine his astonishment when he suddenly beheld his father ! He asked him a thousand questions as to how he had managed to find his way, but the old gentleman calmly replied, ' I told you I should have no difficulty in finding you.' He was never able to understand that it had been a chance in a million to meet an acquaintance of his son's in the first person he addressed. He always maintained that he had known what he was about.

No wonder that Marie and I enjoyed to the full all

the kindness that was shown us on our visit to England —that we loved the country, the people, and everything English. But our greatest happiness was the reception given to our mother wherever she appeared ; she won every heart, was idolised, the audiences could never do enough to show their affection and enthusiasm. How happy I felt, when from my seat in the stalls I saw her making her way to the piano amidst loud applause through the crowded ranks of the shilling seats on the platform, looking round the hall with her kind eyes and bowing acknowledgment ; never forgetting the enthusi- asts at her back who had paid dearly for their seats by long hours of waiting ! When she had sat down at the piano, all the faces were lighted up from the moment when she began to play : then at the end, when she was not allowed to depart before she had been called back again and again, was it not natural that my heart should beat higher, that I was proud of being her child ?

Marie had not quite such an easy time as I had. A thousand little duties fell to her share on concert days. She helped my mother to dress, adorned her smooth, silky hair with black lace and charming velvet flowers, and stayed with her to the last moment. Then she was often so excited that she did not feel like sitting in the stalls with us, but took up her seat in the passage that led to the platform in St. James's Hall, or went with her *passe-partout* from Mr. Chappell to the back of the hall or up to the gallery to hear the effect of the instru- ment which my mother was playing. With a wish to help Erards, who had been very hard hit by the war, my mother had consented to play their instruments alter- nately with Broadwood's. Only those who know the enormous difference in touch which these two makes of pianos require can fully realise what this meant.

When the concert was over and we were all together again at the Burnands' house, where we usually arrived in two carriages, it was touching to see the genuine pleasure of our hosts. Miss Burnand beamed ; she loved my mother beyond all else. Her brother would tell us what observations he had made during the concert : how Miss H. had broken her fan applauding on her programme ; how the ' Old Lady,' an unknown person who always succeeded in getting into the same shilling seat in the front row of the platform, had waved her pocket-handkerchief, while other ladies had stolidly knitted all through the evening ; that George Eliot and George Lewes had been in their usual places in the front row of the stalls. He calculated what profits Chappell must have made on the concert ; had ascertained how many people had been turned away from the doors for want of room. In short, his conversation, pleasant because it showed so much interest, led us back into the ordinary, everyday mood.

I have not said nearly enough in praise of these kind and lovable people, who had made an end once and for all of my mother's staying in lodgings, and surrounded her during these months of onerous work with all the charm of home comforts and freedom from care. Nothing was left undone that love could devise ; all her habits and preferences were studied, and exigencies demanded by her profession were taken into account. The house, the servants, were hers for the time being ; our hosts compressed their own lives into the smallest possible compass, and demanded nothing in return but that we should be happy with them. This was indeed friendship such as will rarely be found, and our hearts have not forgotten it.

Many years later I myself made my home in England. During my twenty years of sojourn, and meeting chiefly with English people, I came to know the country and the nation well, especially as the period of my stay included such important events as the Boer War, the ' Isolation of Germany ' policy, and the Feminist Movement. I no longer found the people I had loved and admired in my youth. Their aristocratic self-confidence which we Germans had envied them had turned to distrustful stand-offishness, their ' Live and let live ' to suspicion of the rising German nation. Even in 1871 we had now and then seen a shade of displeasure pass over the face of an Englishman when our victories were announced. In her diary of January the twenty-seventh, and in a letter to Brahms of the fifth of February, my mother speaks of anti-German feeling. But these impressions were like mists, they did not remain in our memory. Nevertheless, the mists coalesced, became clouds, thickened, and I saw them grow to monstrous proportions. They threatened our very existence; coupled with French hatred, they prepared for our annihilation. I had forebodings of our misfortune. It broke over us more terrible than I had imagined. The time has not yet come to pass a final judgment ; our wounds are still sore, and are being kept open. But I must say this : deeply grieved as I was at the daily widening gulf between the two nations, I gained a price-less possession, and that was, German born and bred, I became doubly a German in England, German by choice, by inmost persuasion, from love of all things German. Only on foreign soil were these ties with the Fatherland fully realised and treasured by me.

If I have lingered in my memory over my first visit to England, it was because it is sweet in these bitter times to recall the days when differences between nations were not stressed ; when art had power to unite, and every-thing that was enjoyable was welcomed in both countries without prejudice. I feel constrained to speak once more of those of both nations who nobly and with true affection gave, and nobly received.

BRAHMS

I

IN the spring of 1872 my mother told me that she was going to ask Brahms to give me lessons during the summer. She thought that the stimulating influence of a fresh teacher might incite me to a more eager pursuit of my studies. I felt very unhappy ; Mamma could not be satisfied with my progress, and I thought that I had done my best. There was no one for whom I would have worked rather than for her. Now Brahms really did come twice a week. He entered the room punctually to the minute, and he was always kind, always patient, and adapted his teaching to my capabilities and the stage of my progress in quite a wonderful way. Also he took a great deal of trouble in the training of my fingers. He had thought about such training and about technique in general much more than my mother, who had surmounted all technical difficulties at an age when one is not yet conscious of them. He made me play a great many exercises, scales and arpeggios as a matter of course, and he gave special attention to the training of the thumb, which, as many will remember, was given a very prominent part in his own playing. When the thumb had to begin a passage, he flung it on to the key with the other fingers clenched. As he kept his wrist loose at the same time, the tone remained full and round even in a fortissimo. Considerable time was daily given to the following exercises on the passing-under of the thumb :—

Also to be played in triplets.

I had to take the note on which the thumb was used, quite lightly—so to speak, on the wing—and accentuate the first of every four notes strongly. Then I had to play the same exercise in triplets, with strong accents on the first note of every triplet. When I could play the exercises faultlessly in keys without the black notes, I played

them, always beginning with the thumb, in C sharp,
F sharp, A flat, E flat, and D flat.

Then followed the common chords with inversions
through three or four octaves, also in groups of four notes
and in triplets, beginning with the accent on the first
note. When I had played this about ten times, I changed
the accent to the second, then to the third note of each
group, so that all the fingers were exercised equally. I
practised these arpeggios alternately as triplets and groups
of six, and had to distinguish clearly between the groups
of twice three and three times two notes.

Brahms made me practise shakes also in triplets. In all exercises he made me play the non-accentuated notes very lightly. I practised the chromatic scale with the first and third, first and fourth, and first and fifth fingers, and he often made me repeat the two consecutive notes where the thumb was passed under. They were all, in fact, quite simple exercises; but carefully executed, first slowly, then more rapidly, and at last prestissimo, I found them extremely helpful for the strengthening, suppleness, and control of the fingers. I also played some of the difficult exercises published later as ' Fifty-one Exercises for Pianoforte by Brahms,' in which he did not include the easier and musically less valuable ones.

With regard to studies Brahms said : play easy ones, but play them as rapidly as possible. He thought very highly of Clementi's ' Gradus ad Parnassum,' and made me play a great number of these.

In the study of Bach's works Brahms laid the greatest stress on rhythm, and gave me directions which, like seeds, took root and continued their growth throughout my musical life. They greatly increased my perception of the subtleties of rhythmic movement. He made it one of the principal rules that in constantly recurring figures the accents should always be the same, and that they should be stressed not so much by strong attack as by greater pressure on the accentuated and more light-ness of the non-accentuated notes.

The melodic notes of figures he made me play lega-tissimo ; the harmonic, however, e.g. the notes of broken chords, quite lightly. He never wrote purely rhythmic accents in above the notes, as he held them to be an integral part of the figure ; but accents specially intended,

JOHANNES BRAHMS
IN 1869

or not self-evident, he marked, to make them quite clear, and pencilled phrasing in with slurs. But I was never allowed to interpret a passage thus phrased by lifting and fresh attack of the hands ; only by rhythmic emphasis and nuance.

Brahms gave much attention to syncopations. They had to be given their full value, and where they produced dissonances with the other parts he made me listen to the syncopated in relation to each one of the dissonant notes. He made the suspensions equally interesting to me ; I could never play them emphatically enough to please him. Of all the works which I studied with Brahms I enjoyed the French Suites most ; it was pure joy to work at them in this way, and he made me see things which I had hitherto passed without noticing, and of which I never again lost sight.

In any work by Bach, Brahms would occasionally permit an emphatic lifting of the notes (portamento), but never a staccato. ' You must not play Bach staccato,' he said to me. ' But Mamma sometimes uses a staccato in Bach,' I demurred. Then he replied, ' Your mother's youth goes back to a time when it was the fashion to use staccatos in Bach, and she has retained them in a few cases.'

Brahms did not give me many directions with regard to the interpretation of the Suites ; he confined himself to explanations of their rhythm and the simplest rules for nuances. ' Play away, play away,' he would call out from time to time in a quick movement.

In the course of the summer I studied with him three French Suites, several Preludes and Fugues from the second book of the Wohltemporierte Klavier, some pieces by Scarlatti, an almost unknown Sonata by Mozart in F major, Variations on a theme in F major by Beethoven (each of which was in a different key), his 32 Variations in C minor, Variations in B flat (Impromptu) by Schubert, some of Mendelssohn's Songs without Words, and Chopin's

Nocturnes. If I remember rightly, nothing of my father's. I must confess to my disgrace that I enjoyed of all these things only the Suites, the C minor Variations, and the Songs without Words ; all the others I hated. I had revelled in my father's G minor Sonata the previous winter, and now I was expected to play all these queer, unexciting pieces. I have often wondered why Brahms made just this selection ? Perhaps he wanted me to form my own judgment on things which I had never heard my mother play, in which I had no tradition to go upon, and thought it would be good for me to become more independent, more self-reliant. This I did to a certain degree, although the results did not show at the time. An almost fatalistic hopelessness with regard to my musical capabilities clogged my progress from the very beginning, lamed the tender wings which might otherwise perhaps have carried me a little higher. Later on I saw how much some of our pupils with moderate gifts achieved by sheer perseverance. But this would not have satisfied me either. I can truthfully say that I have never, positively never, played a single piece to my own satisfaction. I could not play like my mother, and yet I could not play differently, because her playing was my highest ideal, for ever immovably fixed before my eyes. When she found fault with me I was in despair ; when she praised me I burst into tears, saying that she must have a lower standard for me than for herself, else she could not praise what I did. She once said on an occasion like this, ' You forget that I gave my life to music from my earliest childhood.' This touching modesty made me smile, and I said, ' Ah, if I had ten lives and gave them all, I should never play ten bars as you do ! '

I thought it natural that my mother should devote time and strength to me, and it made me happy. But I have never got over the fact that I strummed to Brahms for a whole long summer, and, though in later years he often kindly urged me to play to him again, I could never bring myself to do so. But the seed which he sowed fell upon good soil and bore fruit in the course of years, and when I began to teach I recognised how much I owed to him. I only wish I had told him this.

If I might venture upon comparison between my mother's teaching and his, I would say : My mother primarily stimulated imagination and feeling, Brahms the intellect. To have been influenced by both was perhaps the most perfect teaching imaginable.

One day, shortly before my lesson, Mamma said to Marie and me, ' Children, what has been wrong between you and Brahms ? He complains that you are not nice to him.' We were indignant, said we had always been nice and did not know what he meant. ' Well, ask him yourselves ; I believe he is coming directly.' ' If he is offended,' we said, ' he will probably not come.' But he came, punctually at eleven. We hustled him into a corner, barred the way, and said, ' Now, Herr Brahms, we want to know what the trouble is ; we shall not let you out till you tell us. You have complained of us to Mamma.'

He looked like a dear schoolboy in disgrace, put both his hands in his pockets, shifted his feet, and stammered, ' Oh, it is only because I am such an ass.'

We could not expect a more complete surrender, and were quite touched. We let him out of his corner, and were friends again. We never heard what it was that had hurt his feelings, and thought no more about it.

We children all liked Brahms, but we treated him as one who had always been there, and this perhaps made us a little perfunctory in manner towards him. We took for granted that he was one of the family, and did not take much notice of him. As a composer we thought very highly of him, and emulated his warmest admirers in love for his compositions. We were in raptures about his Serenades and Sextets, and never tired of playing them as piano duets. But it would never have occurred

to us, at least to me, in those days to show these feelings
before him. With regard to the musicians who came
and went in our house I was as much of a fatalist as
about my playing. It would never have entered my
mind that a single one of them could take an interest in
me, or cared for my approval, my understanding or
pleasure in his works. It never occurred to me that
they were human beings like us, that they had human
sides as well as the musical, and looked in others for them.
They were Mamma's property, body and soul, and we
others were there merely by chance. Once the tender
shoot of a friendship was beginning to grow between me
and a young musician. This was dear Liesl von Herzogenberg. Then she came to know my mother, and I
at once retired into the background, as though that were
the most natural thing in the world. Later in life I
learnt how mistaken I was in taking these things for
granted, and I distinctly remember the moment when
this conviction came to me. It was in Leipzig : Brahms
had been playing the pianoforte part in his G minor
Quartet at the Gewandhaus, and at the supper which
followed the concert I was placed next to him. My
heart was so full of the wonderful music that my mouth
overflowed and I said, ' How happy you must have felt
when you completed that quartet ! ' Then he gave me
a beautiful look, such as I have rarely received from him,
and it opened my eyes to the mistake I had made.

I see from Mamma's diary that Brahms took an
interest in Marie's and Elise's musical development when
they were still children. Once he taught them the
' Bilder aus Osten.' They had wanted to give my mother,
who was travelling, a surprise on her return, but could
not manage the pieces alone, so Marie wrote a little note
to Brahms asking for his help, and he came at once.
He seems to have assisted them on other occasions, and
taken an interest in their little concerns. Marie told me
that once when she had accompanied him on a long walk

and chattered all the time, he bought her a lovely Easter egg when they returned to the town. Another time he brought her a book of blank pages with a clasp, bound in leather. He had inscribed the first page with :

POEMS BY MARIE SCHUMANN.

JOH. BRAHMS.
DDORF—*March*, '54.

And the second page with :

> ' Let who will and can pour forth
> Melodies from ev'ry tree.
> There is room for many birds
> In the woods of poetry.'

He did not add on this occasion that the little poetess might improve her handwriting, but he told my mother, who passed on his criticism. His gifts of books to her, such as *Paul and Virginie,* showed not only his kind interest in the child, but also what interested him. The dedications in books which he gave to our mother reflect a part of their lives, and I am often deeply moved when I turn over their pages.

The child Marie grew up and became housekeeper in her mother's household, ever watchful that no comforts should be lacking to our friends, always prepared to provide them with a meal, so that they should ' stretch forth their hands to the good cheer spread before them.' Brahms gave her at that time a cookery-book with a dedication, and adorned with charming and quaint colour prints and rhymes.

When he gave presents they made one feel that he had carefully selected them with a view to giving real pleasure. For this, naturally, an understanding of the recipient's inclinations and tastes was necessary. But whatever can he have meant by a birthday present which he once gave me many years later ? He was staying with us in Frankfurt, and had heard in the morning that it was my birthday. When we went in to dinner, I found beside my plate a prettily modelled donkey in silver bronze which carried on its back—of all things—a little liqueur barrel with glasses all complete. Was that also due to a study of my habits? I am not sure that it was not! Of course, I was teased a great deal about it, but I was quite pleased with my present; I knew he would not have given it to me had he not liked it himself.

Brahms was very fond of teasing, and Marie, who was not at all touchy and always prepared to join in a laugh against herself, was usually the butt of his humour. Once he said at dinner, 'Well, Fräulein Marie, to-day you were in the mood again when no Beethoven sonata was good enough for you.' When we looked at them in surprise, he confessed that he always walked up and down in front of the cottage to the last moment before dinner for fear of being caught in a cross-fire between two pianos, and that he had heard Marie strum the beginning of one sonata after another.

Once our cook was ill, our dear, kind Josephine, whom I have never forgotten because Mamma and Marie were inconsolable at losing her. As we could not at once find a substitute, Marie had to do the cooking. Brahms made a point of praising her dishes, and once, when he had particularly enjoyed one of them, he said impulsively, 'Well, now, I shall look and see whether you have really kept strictly to the recipe,' ran to the bookshelf, took the cookery-book and read, 'Take . . . There! I thought so! an onion; I never noticed the onion; I am sure you left that out.' He said he did not like Marie's bread-fritters: 'I 've eaten better.' This shows that the educational element was not lacking, and it was not merely one-sided. For instance, the sisters insisted on his folding up his table napkin after dinner; he quickly learnt to manage the proper folding, but in rolling he would always turn the seams outside.

Undoubtedly Brahms felt more at his ease with Marie

than with us other 'Fräuleins,' as he called us. Her equable, kindly temperament, the friendliness with which she met all our visitors, created an atmosphere in which every one felt at ease. For Brahms, our mother's beloved friend, she naturally had a particularly tender spot in her heart, and never failed to show him the kindest attention, anticipating his every wish from the time of our first summer in Baden to his last visit in Frankfurt in 1895. She told me again recently that he was the most considerate and frugal of guests in a modest household.

He treated Elise as a good comrade; this was congenial both to his temperament and to hers. She was, however, rarely with us. He had had an admiration for Julie from the time when, as a girl of sixteen, she had accompanied our mother on a concert tour to Hamburg. His admiration grew as she developed in more and more exquisite loveliness, and in the summer of 1869, when she was just engaged, and brimful of vitality, I often saw his eyes shining when he looked at her. I do not venture to guess how near his feelings came to the passion of real devotion. Perhaps Julie's self-possessed, unvarying friendliness towards him had excluded a deeper affection from the first.

He also took a warm interest in our brothers; but as they were sent to school early, and at last quite disappeared from our circle, he did not often have an opportunity of showing it. It was a great grief to him to see our mother suffer because of their tragic fate, without being able to help her in any way. Once when she complained how much sorrow she had to bear in her sons, he said, 'At any rate, you are very fortunate in your daughters.' Although I failed to see how that could really comfort my mother, I was glad Brahms should have such a good opinion of us, and hoped that a little of it might fall to my share.

II

I did not know at that time what Brahms's friendship
had meant to my mother during the most tragic time of
her life. It was not till several years after her death that
I read the words which she had written in her diary and
left to us as a last will and testament—words binding us
to lifelong gratitude towards the friend who had sacrificed
years of his young life to her. But I could and did understand what his existence meant to her, what he, and only
he, could give her. It was Brahms to whom after our
father's death she owed the supreme joy of still being
able to follow step by step the creative musician's art.
She had tasted this joy from childhood upwards ; had
developed with the creations of Chopin, Mendelssohn, and
Schumann. Her own beloved had led her deeply into
the spirit of Bach's and Beethoven's works. Now it was
Brahms whom she accompanied on his course, whose
genius lent her wings to soar. She once asked me if I
could at all realise what it meant to have had a friend from
childhood upwards who stimulated all your noblest and
most artistic qualities, who in daily and hourly intercourse
lavished pearls and jewels upon you ; if I did not think
it natural that she felt she could not go on living deprived
of such gifts, and that she clung to friends like Brahms and
Joachim who could console her in some measure for what
she had lost. She said she could never have borne her
sorrows without the loving efforts of these friends to
bring her back to music.

Yes, indeed, we could realise it ! We knew that in
our mother woman and artist were indissolubly one, so
that we could not say this belongs to one part of her and
that to another. We would sometimes wonder whether
our mother would miss us or music most if one of the
two were taken from her, and we could never decide.
We were thankful that Brahms had been sent her as a
companion. We also knew that he was devoted to her

with his whole soul, that in spite of his brusque ways he loved and admired her more than any one else in the world. All their differences ended in their clasping hands again, for their friendship rested on the rock of deep mutual understanding and unanimity in all that is deepest and truest in life and in art.

The cause of their differences lay in Brahms's uncompromising manner and my mother's extreme sensitiveness, which would sometimes see things out of proportion. She had had love lavished upon her all her life, and her soft, affectionate heart could not bear unkind words or blunt manners from those she loved. She well understood the artistic temperament with its moods ; years of experience had taught her what it meant when ' the iron was in flux,' as Brahms once wrote to her. She was prepared to pay the price which the creative genius has a right to exact from the world, indulgence during the time of creativeness. She could understand withdrawal into oneself, taciturnity, irritability ; but she could not understand—for it was foreign to her own nature—the visiting of sullen moods upon others in personal hurt.

It is difficult to decide how much of Brahms's brusqueness was natural disposition, or how far life had developed it in him. It is certain that my mother and other friends had been made to feel it even in the early Düsseldorf days, and it comes out occasionally in the first letters to my mother. But on the other hand these give proof of so warm a heart, so much tender sympathy, that one cannot but ascribe to outward circumstances the callousness with which he could wound his friends' feelings. His genius, the bent of his nature, were in striking contrast to the environment into which he was born. He himself told my mother that as a mere boy he saw things and received impressions which left a deep shadow on his mind. Afterwards he had known happy times also. He won the friendship of Joachim, then that of my parents ; and when my father had been stricken with

153

illness, his whole soul was filled with devotion to my mother, to which he had—not sacrificed, for he followed the call of his heart, but consecrated several years of his life. But it was inevitable he should recognise that the destiny which he had to fulfil was irreconcilable with single-minded devotion to a friendship. To recognise this and immediately seek a way out was the natural outcome of his virile nature. That he broke away ruthlessly was perhaps also an inevitable consequence when one takes his inherent qualities and the nature of the situation into account. But without doubt he had had a hard struggle with himself before he had steered his craft in a fresh direction, and he had never got over the self-reproach of having wounded my mother's feelings at the time, and felt that this could never be undone. This consciousness often made him appear harsh ; at least, we children have explained it thus. Their friendship had been put to a hard test ; it was the best proof of its immortality that it had survived it. My mother had suffered all the more as she could not understand the change in him. Her own mind and heart were laid down on such clear and simple lines that she could not enter into the more complex processes of the human soul. She remained towards Brahms what she had always been ; she loved him truly and whole-heartedly. Her feelings for him might have been those of a mother for her son, if admiration had not so strongly predominated. The admiration she felt for the artist was also bestowed on the man. She could as little think of Brahms the man and Brahms the artist as separate entities as she could separate the woman from the artist in herself. She certainly was right ! If only she had been able to understand the man as well as she understood the artist ! She could see the ruggedness in his compositions, especially the earlier ones, without losing her admiration for the work thereby ; but when the ruggedness of his nature came out in his manner to her, it hurt her deeply. Sometimes she would even take offence where, I am sure, none was meant. I used to take his part on these occasions, if only to calm and comfort her, and she would then say, ' You don't know what he was like formerly, so full of tender and delicate feeling, an ideal person.' I wonder whether he had really been as different as she thought, or whether she had seen him differently ? A man of twenty-five is of course different from one of thirty-five ; life is a hardening process ; with the good the less good qualities become established in a measure as experiences and ambitions exert their influence upon them. Understanding of the creative artist's soul makes one indulgent towards him. His is a life of eternal stress and strain ; he is the slave of the elusive goddess of inspiration, she never lets him rest. However great the gifts which he has just bestowed upon the world, he may not breathe freely. No sooner has he laboured to produce one work, than new ideas for the next are beginning to stir and urgently demand to be brought to light. And when hours of doubt of his own genius come to an artist—and Brahms was spared these no more than others—life may become a veritable hell.

I am sure that Brahms suffered more than he made others suffer by his faults. He may sometimes have relieved his feelings momentarily by an outburst, but it did not make him happy ; on the contrary, he hurt his own heart. His ruggedness was a perpetual state of defence against suspected attacks of others on his independence and the privacy of his existence. If you took his opinion on anything for granted, he invariably put himself in opposition. If, however, he felt that you genuinely wanted his instruction and had some matter at heart, he could enter very kindly into the subject. I remember telling him once that I was very anxious to form my own judgment on Wagner's operas. He listened kindly and patiently, so that I was encouraged to tell him at length what impressions I had received of the

'Trilogy,' 'Tristan,' etc. Then he said, 'Have you heard the "Flying Dutchman"? No? Be sure to hear it; that is the best thing Wagner has done.' Another time I wrote and asked him how pupils could best be taught transposing. This too he answered kindly in a letter to my mother in August 1894 : 'Fräulein Eugenie might have been certain that I would have written to her by return and at length if I had had anything useful to say about instruction in transposing. But I think it is chiefly a matter of practice and habit. Daily accompanying of singers will soon make you learn it, and I should recommend this primarily. Also valses, easy Haydn symphonies, etc. The principal thing is to acquire a quick grasp and ease in the treatment of it. Thorough knowledge of harmony is of course very useful, but I cannot understand what benefit any one would derive from years of study in harmony.'

Superficial or curious inquirers were, however, treated mercilessly by Brahms. Whenever he suspected their intention he snubbed them with an ambiguous answer or a frivolous joke. Although he loved human intercourse and sought it, he was always on the defensive when he was sought after. He liked to give, but resented demands or expectations. He selected his friends very carefully, and there were not many who passed muster. Once, during the last years of his life, he went so far as to say in an outburst of moodiness, 'I have no friends ; if any one tells you he is my friend, don't believe him !' We were speechless. At last I said, 'But, Herr Brahms, friends are the best gift in this world. Why should you resent them?' He looked at me with wide-open eyes and did not reply. Brahms undoubtedly has suffered much. He was very human, as human as one can be, and that is why he was also loved much.

No wonder that we were often angry with him when he hurt our mother's feelings in a bad humour. He could be rude to all and sundry at times, without exceptions that I know of. That was not our concern—others must look after themselves. But our mother ! We could not bear it, and would sometimes tell him what we thought. ' No, Herr Brahms, you have no business to speak to Mamma like that,' I once cried, kneeling down by her, whose eyes had filled with tears. He again looked at me half surprised, half startled, but in silence. I never could understand how his own kind heart could let him hurt my mother's. There was a small demon in him, and who does not know from experience that we are apt to let it off against those of whose affection we can always be sure ? This was the case with him. What Brahms loved in our mother above everything, above even her artistic understanding, was her great heart ; he could be sure of its love and forgiveness even if he were to let loose a legion of demons. It was character-istic of their relations that Brahms, who could be unkind to her himself, never allowed any one else, not even us, to find fault with her. Once when we were alone with him in the dining-room, and Mamma had just been called away, one of us said, ' Really, Mamma has not got a single fault.' ' Yes,' another answered, ' I can think of one fault. When there has been some disagreement among us and I tell her my side of it, she agrees with me ; and when the other one goes and tells her, she agrees with her.' Brahms turned to the last speaker and said, ' You are overlooking that this fault is in reality one of her virtues. Your mother is so modest that she never absolutely insists on her opinion, not even to you.'

I liked to look at Brahms when he said, ' Your mother.' The blue of his eyes showed at its purest and softest. We children loved in Brahms his fresh, youth-ful virility, his thoroughly German characteristics, his genuineness and reliability, the clarity of his mind which saw and made others see things as they were. But above all we loved him for his love for our mother. Whatever else I may have come to doubt in the course of my life,

I have never doubted Brahms's loyalty. And if to him her great heart was the strongest attraction, she too knew that her friend had a heart that understood every emotion of hers and would be devoted to her to the end of her days.

III

The long months of intercourse with Brahms came to an end when we sold our dear cottage on the borders of the Oos and no longer spent the summers in it. We went to live in Berlin, which Brahms did not like ; he therefore only came for a few days from time to time to see Mamma, but never for a longer stay. We still met in Baden, which had once more attracted us in the summer; and later in other holiday resorts. Twice we visited him, once in Ziegelhausen on the Neckar, once in Nildbad near Zurich. In both places he had taken in a farmhouse two or three nice rooms with many windows and little furniture. They showed how few were his needs as regards comfort, but what he did need was a lavish supply of air and light, and room to pace up and down.

In January 1877, when we were again thinking of moving, Brahms wrote, ' Think seriously about L(eipzig). If you went there I should probably—decidedly—go there too for the winter months. There are many charming people there.' And again at the end of the letter, ' Best greetings to the children, and talk a lot about Leipzig at breakfast.' The ' charming people ' were principally Heinrich and Liesl von Herzogenberg, who would have been delightful to live with in any place. Mamma had many other friends in Leipzig, but in spite of this she could not make up her mind to return permanently to her native town, and accepted an offer from Frankfurt for a wide field of activity at the new Conservatoire of Music which had been founded by Dr. Hoch. While we were preparing to move there in the summer of

1878, I received a letter from Brahms, to my great astonishment. What could it be about ?

'Pörtschach on the Lake, Carinthia.

'May I ask you, dear friend, to give me your help in perpetrating a little practical joke ?

'I possess a few sheets of music with your mother's maiden name ; they are evidently fragments of early compositions of hers. I should like to excite your mother's interest in them, and to know if she has got another copy, if the things have been published, or if she would still complete them from memory ?

'It would serve my purpose best if I were to send you the sheets, and you told her or wrote to her that you had found them among other things during the move.

'The point is that I do not want your mother to toss them aside as of no importance, and if you were going to Baden to her you could help to make her interested in them.

'At present I only want to know whether this letter has found you, and where I may send the music. After that I should like a very full account of how you succeed and what happens.—With kindest regards, your

'J. Brahms.

'*June* 1878.'

For the sake of coherence in this little story I give my answer also :—

'Frankfurt, 23 *June* 1878.

'Dear Herr Brahms !—What a pity that you did not write a few days earlier ! It is now impossible to perpetrate the little fraud, for Mamma has been here since yesterday, and we shall be leaving Frankfurt the day after to-morrow for the whole summer. But perhaps you could send us the sheets in the autumn ? There are still a great many boxes of music to be unpacked, and we should have every opportunity of making a nice little discovery. If

we can only persuade Mamma to complete the pieces !
It will not be easy, but we will try.

' Mamma is going to Munich on Tuesday with Marie ;
will stay there for a day or two and then go on to Gastein.
I am meeting my better half in Vienna, whence we shall
start for a holiday in the Austrian mountains.

' I should like to tell you how your Symphony again
delighted me when I heard it in Düsseldorf. It was the
one really enjoyable feature of the festival. "Faust" had
not been sufficiently well rehearsed, and " Orfeo " is too
dull, although Marie tells me I must not say such a thing.

' Now good-bye, dear Herr Brahms. Shall we not
meet this summer ? Every one in Düsseldorf was grieved
at your absence. If one did not owe so much to the
solitary places which you seek, one would bear them a
grudge.—With kindest remembrances, yours,

' EUGENIE SCHUMANN.'

I imagined that the matter would end there. With
my better half, Marie Fillunger, I had accepted an
invitation to Castle Habrowan, near Bratislava, Herr and
Frau von Gomperz's residence. We spent delightful
weeks with them, and made firm friends with our hostess,
who had been well known on the operatic stage under
her maiden name of Bettelheim. No restraints were put
upon the guests ; every one was at liberty to do as he
pleased ; only meals and music united us all in the lofty
rooms of the castle. We often had the pleasure of hearing
our hostess's rich alto in duets with my friend's soprano.
I loved our wanderings through field-paths. For the first
time in my life I realised the beauty of cornfields—and
what cornfields they were, these of the Hanna Plains !
Far as the eye could reach there was a sea of bending
ears ; I no more tired of looking at them than one tires
of looking at the sea. There was something touching in
the thought that year after year human labour wakes
this spectacle to life. In spite of our long summers in

Baden and other country places, I was really town-bred, and only now learnt from my charming hostess the difference between wheat and rye, oats and barley. A kind wind wafted me another letter from Brahms across this golden glory one day :—

'DEAR FRÄULEIN EUGENIE,—I cannot help it, the matter cannot be left to stand over till the autumn; and although you are abruptly breaking off diplomatic relations and retiring to a mountain fastness, I am trying to find you, so as to smuggle into your hands the valuable documents I have of your mother's industry.

'Now please do me the favour of sending them to your mother. If you really *had* found them in Berlin, it would have been wrong to drag them about in the desert. Then let me know the report, and what your mother's face looks like in her letter.

'But you might in any case have written and told me where you are spending your holidays. I sometimes go for walks in the Austrian mountains, and it would be a pity to pass you and your better half or any other half.

'My best thanks for your kind praises. That is the kind of thing one likes to hear, even if it is at the expense of a valued colleague—the Chevalier Gluck, to boot.

'As I hope to have more to write presently, I will only recommend myself to you and the above-mentioned half very sincerely as yours,   J. BRAHMS.

'PÖRTSCHACH ON THE LAKE, CARINTHIA,
    '*beginning of July* 1878.'

'HABROWAN, 15 *July* 1878.

'DEAR HERR BRAHMS !—At last we have advanced a little, but I do not know if the result will be to your satisfaction. I sent the music to Mamma with a carefully prepared lie which I beg you to take upon your conscience, and I am copying out her answer exactly :—

'"With the exception of one bit which sounded a little Brahmsish-Hungarian, the composition was entirely new

161

to me, but Brahms, who has looked through every rag of paper I possess, will probably be able to say where it belongs. Some parts sound to me like Schumann, others like Brahms, but now and then I feel as if I myself might have written them. Well, I suppose the mystery will be cleared up by and by."

' This is what Mamma writes. Marie's report is enclosed. I am afraid the result will not satisfy you, but I do not know what you are driving at. If I can still be of use in the matter, please count on me for further frauds.

' Fillu and I have been staying here for the last fortnight with Herr and Frau von Gomperz. It has been a great pleasure to make their acquaintance, for they are very charming people. But to-morrow we are leaving for the Prein in the Lower Austrian Hills, where we intend to stay for several weeks. How nice it would be if you really were to surprise us there one day ! but you will hardly extend your walks so far.

' I hope you will find it possible to spend a month with Mamma in the autumn. Apart from everything else it would be a comfort to us to know that she has your help in the revision of the new edition, which excites her more than is good for her.

' Now good-bye, dear Herr Brahms. Best greetings from Fillu and yours very sincerely,

' EUGENIE SCHUMANN.'

Extract from Marie's Letter to Eugenie.

' WILDBAD GASTEIN, 12 *July* 1878.

' . . . You will have been waiting for news of the reception which your MS. had. Well, there is not much to say. Mamma had hardly looked at the sheets when she said, " I never wrote that—some one must have used my paper and sketched out something on it." When we came to the part of your letter where you intended to take her in, she did not seem to know what to make of it . . . of course I made her play the pieces through next day, and she said, "That is quite uncommon, but I did not write it; it might be by Papa, or some of it might be Brahms. I must ask him; he knows every bit of paper that we possess."

'I should have liked her to send off the sheets to him at once for the fun of it, but she said, "He would think it ridiculous of me to write to him on account of such a trifle; I'll show it to him some day."'

As I said before, I did not know what the point of Brahms's joke was. Shortly afterwards he visited Mamma in Gastein, and it turned out that his intention had been to trap her. She still possessed some sheets of very pretty notepaper stamped with her maiden name. Brahms had taken some of these and commissioned some one to copy out on them parts of his newest compositions for piano. He had intended that our mother should take them for early compositions of her own, but, as I have explained, he had not succeeded. My mother wrote to me on July 25, 'Brahms has completed the two pieces very beautifully, and three others to go with them.' Probably they are those which appeared as Piano Pieces, op. 76, in 1879.

My mother could easily be taken in in ordinary life, and Brahms usually succeeded in his little hoaxes; but it was a very different matter when it came to music. Once he told her he had written a new piano concerto, of which he would play her the first movement; sat down forthwith and played away. When he had finished, Mamma looked at him, smiled, and said, 'Do you think you can make me believe that that is a piano concerto? Not a bit of it! It is a symphony.' And so it was.

In September 1882 we were in Bellagio with Mamma, and Brahms came with Billroth[1] to be with her on her

---

[1] Famous surgeon.

birthday, the thirteenth. We had intended to go to Venice together on the fifteenth, when we were hoping to meet the Herzogenbergs. Then rain set in, such as I cannot recollect to have often seen. The clouds were bursting and the lake was covered with high waves. The gentlemen said that it was impossible to start in such weather. But we had packed, arranged everything, ordered rooms in Milan and Venice, and were determined to go through with it. Our friends said good-bye to us, and promised to follow on the next day. The crossing to Como was terrible, and the passage from the boat to the train still worse. I had occasion once more to admire our mother, who, nervous by nature, could be heroic when the moment demanded it. We arrived safely in Milan. Next morning we went on, still in pouring rain, which stopped towards mid-day. When we were near Verona, proceeding at a terrific speed towards the railway bridge, we saw an enormous crowd of people standing on the banks of the turbid, yellow Adige. They seemed to be gazing horror-struck from the floods to the approaching train. We crossed the bridge, all unconscious of the danger through which we were passing, and only heard on our arrival at Venice that our train had been the last which the bridge had borne ; soon after we had crossed, the furious river had destroyed it.

Our friends were now prevented from joining us on the next day. Our regrets were not unmixed with a little malice because of their shyness of rain. I do not remember how they managed to reach Venice, for the main connection by Verona was interrupted for many weeks ; but four days later, when we were sitting on the Piazza drinking our coffee, they suddenly appeared, with their clothes dry but their spirits somewhat damped. They sat down, and we exchanged notes of our experiences. Brahms was in one of his worst moods, and Billroth had no doubt had his share of it, for when we got up he offered Marie one arm and me the other and confided his troubles to us in undertones. Nothing he did had been right. He invited Mamma and us, who were staying at the Pension Anglaise, to dine with them at his hotel the next day. Brahms, who never let anything escape him, and who had no doubt noticed our confidential talk with Billroth, took us aside and said perhaps we would like to know that the next day was Billroth's birthday. Of course, we were glad to know it, for we had taken a great liking to the charming, distinguished native of the beautiful Island of Rügen, and to his melancholy blue eyes. We discussed what might give him pleasure, and as we had noticed that he was passionately fond of nuts, Marie with her deft fingers made a little bag which we filled with nuts and sent to his hotel with some congratulatory verses. When we arrived, Billroth thanked us most kindly, but added with slight embarrassment that it was not his birthday at all, that Brahms had played another of his tricks on us. This was a harmless one, and interfered in no way with further very pleasant hours. However, he played another trick on us, with good intentions but unpleasant results, on our way from Venice to Udine. Herr and Frau von Herzogenberg were travelling with us. We five had taken our places in a compartment, Brahms and Billroth stood on the platform, when three gentlemen proceeded to get in. 'There is only room for one,' cried Brahms; 'the compartment is full.' 'But there are three seats, just what we want,' said one of the gentlemen. 'No, no,' said Brahms; 'we are going.' We were greatly astonished; the gentlemen were obliged to do the best they could, as the train was on the point of starting and very full. One got in, the others squeezed in where they could. The guard came to close the doors, and of course we expected Brahms and Billroth to get in, but the signal was given and we started. We looked at each other in silence; but silence was not a virtue of our fellow-passenger's. He was in the right, of course, but he relieved his feelings by a perfect flood of abuse which we were quite unable to stem, as he would not even listen to our excuses, and did not believe what he did manage to hear. This overcharged atmosphere was happily cleared at the next station, where he got out and joined his companions.

When we had taken up our abode in Frankfurt, Brahms visited us there every year, and his visits were always stimulating. It was astonishing how full of life the house seemed directly Brahms set foot in it. This was primarily due to the eagerness with which he absorbed and communicated everything of interest. Usually the thing which was uppermost in his mind at the moment came out within the first few hours ; it poured itself forth, and this abundant enthusiasm gave him a touch of boyishness even in his advanced years. Once it was an operation performed by Billroth which he had explained to him, and of which he was so full that he must try to retail it all to us. Another time it was the career of the young singer Wüllner which absorbed his interest. Again that of Dvořák, for whom he had a warm appreciation. One might indeed say that it was he who had discovered him. He tried hard to make my mother like his music, but without success. She maintained her independence of judgment against him as she had maintained it against our father when she had defended Bellini and not cared for Sterndale Bennett. Brahms had all Dvořák's music sent to her ; he played all the piano duets with her, and she looked conscientiously through the other works. She was genuinely glad when in part she could join in her friend's appreciation, but the compositions as a whole did not appeal to her, and she made no secret of it. Brahms, however, has told me himself that he regretted Dvořák's having published many inferior things.

Another time the first thing he said was, ' They are

giving a new piece at the theatre here, " Ehre," by Suder-
mann ; we must go and see it.' That same evening I
took these two big children, Mamma and Brahms, to
the theatre. Poor Mamma could hardly any longer
hear a word of what was spoken on the stage, but her
eyes followed with the greatest interest what was passing;
and her friend's, too, were riveted on the stage. Fitger's
' Hexe ' excited him equally.

He often told us of his travels in Italy ; gave his opinion
on Hans von Bülow, the artist Max Klinger, and others.
Whenever he came to us from Meiningen, he could not
say enough of the artistic life there, of the wonderful
orchestra and his many hours of rehearsal with them ;
of the warm welcome and hours of unrestrained intercourse with his princely host and his consort. He tried to
persuade our mother to accept one of their many invitations to come to Meiningen ; often as the journey had
been planned, however, it never came off.

Brahms shared in all the interests of our home as
warmly as we shared in his. It is general knowledge
that he helped our mother with the revision of our
father's collected works ; but no one except ourselves
knew how much trouble his ever-ready helpfulness saved
her when she had undertaken this responsibility.

He was greatly interested when he heard that Marie
and I had undertaken preparatory classes for our mother.
' The first thing is to get hold of a good School of Pianoforte Playing,' he said, and soon afterwards made us a
present of four volumes of Czerny's, originally published
by Diabelli in Vienna. We set to work at once, and found
so many useful exercises that we wished to make them
more accessible to our pupils in a selected edition. Our
mother at once inquired from the publisher who had
taken the work over from Diabelli if he had brought
out a selection. Herr Cranz in Hamburg answered
that he had not, but would be very pleased if my mother
would undertake an edition, and offered a considerable

sum. She had, however, neither time nor inclination to do so. When we told Brahms of this the next time we saw him, he said to our mother, ' If Marie were to make the selection and I helped her, you would not mind putting your name to it ? ' She agreed, and work was started without delay. Many annotations and excellent suggestions in Brahms's hand in the second volume show how seriously he took the work, and I had another opportunity of verifying the fact that really great artists excel in faithful attention to the minutest detail.

When the work was finished, my mother revised it, and it was subsequently published under the title of ' Exercises and Studies from Carl Czerny's Great School of Pianoforte Playing, op. 500. Selected and edited by Clara Schumann. Published by Aug. Cranz.'

Brahms as well as my mother was of opinion that technique, more especially fingering, must be learnt through exercises, so that in the study of pieces attention may be concentrated unhampered upon the spirit of the music. I can say without exaggeration that Beethoven's sonatas and concertos present no difficulties to the student who has mastered these Czerny exercises perfectly in the quickest tempo desired. Modern technicians might object that in these exercises the thumb is hardly ever used on black notes. But this studied avoidance gives great suppleness to the thumb, so that one easily gets accustomed to the use of it on black notes also.

The interest which he took in this work induced Brahms soon afterwards to publish his Fifty-one Exercises, which, as it appeared, he had worked out mostly at an earlier period.

The nicest time of the day used to be breakfast-time. When I came down into the dining-room I saw nothing at first except thick clouds of tobacco smoke, pierced by Mamma's affectionate good-morning glance. Brahms was more difficult to discover, and I read a slight dis-

approval of my late appearance in his look. He was
an early riser, and often used to tell us in Baden, ' You
don't know what you are missing when you are not in
the woods by five o'clock.' I admit that it was a bad
habit to get up so late. Now I am glad of the first rays
of morning light, when I can get up, but at that time I
found it dreadfully hard to get out of bed. The awkward
moment passed, and, kind Marie having given me my
tea, I still managed to catch some of the cosy morning
talk, which embraced large and small interests ; even a
little gossip did not come amiss.

Like all lonely people, Brahms formed his opinions
quietly, and independently of outside influences. He
disliked arguments and evaded them where he could,
but when he was drawn into them he could become
very passionate. This did not happen very often, as
most people admitted his superiority without demur.
He and my mother agreed in most things of real importance, as I have already had occasion to mention. ' Of
course,' he once said with reference to a question of
general interest—' of course I entirely agree with you.
But,' he continued, turning to us, ' your mother is the
only person who can take her stand on a matter like
this openly. Others simply can't do it. If I were to
say about Wagner what she does, the papers would make
a stunt of it, and I would never let myself in for that.
If a newspaper were to print to-day that I had murdered
my father, I wouldn't reply.' This may explain why he
has often answered evasively or even ambiguously questions bearing upon the above-mentioned subject. I will
not presume to judge whether he was right in this.

Our mother was a decided antagonist of Wagner's
music ; she opposed it passionately and with full conviction, not because she was biassed in favour of other
composers, but because she did not see in it a wholesome
development of the art which above all she loved.
Music was the true home of her soul, a materialisation

of everything divine ; it was her religion and her temple, the sanctuary in which it was the only god. She said she would not presume to judge Wagner's importance in art apart from his music, but she could not regard him as a musician like others who believed in music for music's sake. To him it was a means to an end, often an end of mere superficial effect. If this course were followed up, it would mean the ruin of music.

I return, however, to our breakfast-table.

We would often sit talking for a long time, but Marie reminded him sometimes, ' Herr Brahms, you really must practise now, or you will not play properly at the concert.' Then he always got up obediently, went into the music-room with his beloved cigar, and presently we heard the vigorous attack of his two fifth fingers, one at each extreme end of the keyboard, and arpeggios in counter movement through endless modulations followed.

Interesting as this playing was, there was always something of a fight or animosity about it. I do not believe that Brahms looked upon the piano as a dear, trusted friend, as my mother did, but considered it a necessary evil with which one must put up as best one could.

Brahms's visits to us were often connected with first performances of his works at the Museum Concerts. Sometimes he conducted one of his symphonies or overtures, also his Haydn Variations ; sometimes he played the piano part in a chamber-music work. The rehearsals for the latter always took place at our house in the presence of all the notable Frankfurt musicians, so as to give us all the opportunity of hearing them several times and understanding them better. It was a joy to be present at performances of one work after another, and to profit by hearing them played and afterwards discussed. To our mother, who was able to grasp at once the design of each work as a whole, these occasions were a pure joy.

It was not always perfectly enjoyable to hear Brahms play his own compositions, but it was always highly interesting. Marie once characterised his rendering of the B major Concerto as ' a spirited sketch.' He played the themes with great emphasis and curiously free rhythms ; merely outlining everything in the nature of accompanying sections, so that one had the impression of strong light and shade. When he came to passionate parts, it was as though a tempest were tossing clouds, scattering them in magnificent fury. He then made one feel the limits which the instrument imposed upon him. From a purely pianistic point of view his playing was not satisfying ; once I have even heard him play my father's Quartet in E flat major in a most unsatisfactory way. But this did not often occur. In his later years he hardly ever played anything except his own compositions, where he did not mind whether he reached technical perfection or not. One day he played the piano part in his Violin Sonata in D minor at our house. Mamma used to say that there was one bit marked ' tranquillo ' at the end of the third movement, where one walked on eggs. Marie and I were most anxious to hear how he would manage to get safely across. When it came, he took the tranquillo so excessively slowly that nothing could happen. We smiled at each other. ' There he goes tiptoeing over the eggs,' we thought.

Brahms's last visit to us was during the last days of October 1895. He was on his way from Meiningen, and only stayed twenty-four hours. His mood was of the happiest owing to his having been fully appreciated. The evening of his stay with us was made particularly enjoyable by his meeting with intimate old friends, Professor Kufferath from Brussels, his daughter Antonia, her husband Mr. Edward Speyer, and a few others. I remember one of the topics which were discussed at supper, and Brahms's comment. A former pupil of my mother's was going to make his first appearance in

Berlin shortly at an orchestral concert. Some one asked what he was going to play, and the name of a perfectly unknown composer was mentioned. Every one thought it a mistake, and Brahms put the various opinions in a nutshell by saying, ' When you are introducing yourself, you should not introduce another at the same time.'

After supper we asked Antonia to sing. It was always a great joy to hear her. Her singing was exquisitely tender and expressive, and her innate musical sense gave it a security which indeed satisfied the severest demands. She sang several of the Volkslieder : Brahms accompanied. At the end we all asked for our favourite, ' In stiller Nacht.' Brahms has enhanced by a wonderful accompaniment with strange rhythmic device the appeal of this haunting, touching plaint of a heart stricken to death. For the greater part the piano is a quaver in advance of the voice ; although this makes it extraordinarily impressive, it is not easy for the singer, who must have a very true sense of rhythm.

' Can you sing that in time ? ' Brahms asked her.

' I think I can,' she said with a mischievous smile, ' if you can play it in time.'

The next morning I heard Mamma play Prelude and Fugue with Pastorale (both written for organ) by Bach ; then Brahms's Romance in F major and Intermezzo in E flat major, op. 118. A little while after she had finished I went in. Mamma was sitting sideways at her writing-table ; her cheeks were gently flushed and her eyes shone as though illumined by a light from within. Brahms, who was sitting opposite to her, was evidently touched with deep emotion. ' Your mother has been playing most beautifully to me,' he said. I stayed with them, and presently Brahms asked me to find the third volume of Beethoven Sonatas, so that he could look up something. I took what he wanted from Mamma's shelves. He found a particular page, and exclaimed, ' Really, it is wonderful how infallible your mother's ear is ! Look at this note which is printed in every edition of Beethoven's Sonatas. I always thought that it must be a misprint, and when I had an opportunity lately of seeing the sonata in manuscript I found my opinion justified. Now I see that your mother has already corrected it. No other musician has an ear like that.' How specially proud I was of my little mother !

A few hours later Brahms said good-bye. The two friends embraced and kissed as they had done for years at every meeting and parting, but this time there was to be no more meeting. Shortly afterwards my mother fell ill, and in May of the following year she was taken from us. The last time I saw Brahms he was standing by her grave.

While I was writing this chapter the thought, ' What would Brahms say if he read it ? ' came to me again and again. He who hated to be talked or written about. But I felt on the other hand that great men, living or dead, will be written about, and as an irresistible impulse has compelled me to write down what I was able to draw from the well-spring of first-hand, vivid memories, I wished to represent him, our lifelong friend, as I have known him under varying circumstances in intimate intercourse. What I have told of him, to the best of my knowledge and memory, may help others to understand Brahms the man.

He represented to us the finest type of a true German, who never wanted to appear other than he was. The few faults he had were very much in evidence ; he took no trouble to draw aside the slight veil they formed, and left it to others to lift it from the heart of pure gold which was hidden beneath.

BERLIN—FRANKFURT

I

YEARS came and went. Once more, as during my childhood, we spent five years in Berlin (1873-78). We had taken an airy, charming flat in Unter den Zelten ; the trees of the Tiergarten looked in at our windows, and we on our part looked into those of the Joachims, who were living opposite us with their four beautiful children in their own villa. The Stockhausens also were living in Berlin, but in a distant part of the town, so that we could not reach them very easily. Soon after we had taken up our abode there, my mother's half-brother, Musik-Direktor Woldemar Bargiel from Rotterdam, was appointed to a professorship at the new College of Music. This was a great pleasure to us ; he was one of the most musical of musicians, and moreover a man of wide culture. We enjoyed seeing a great deal of him and his kind, very musical wife, a Dutchwoman by birth. They had only one child at that time, a charming little daughter, who had unfortunately lost a leg through a railway accident. The way in which the parents bore this trial, and taught the child to bear it, was touching and admirable. Little Clementine grew up into a brave woman who became a help in every way to her brother and sister, who were ten and twelve years her juniors. We still had, of course, many friends in Berlin ; new ones were now added to the old, and there was no lack of musical intercourse. All the musicians of eminence who either lived in Berlin or spent some time there forgathered at the Joachims', Stockhausens', and our house, when a large number of amateurs from

174

different circles were asked to meet them. I will mention Field-Marshal Count von Moltke as the most notable among these. We had the great pleasure of meeting him at one of the Joachims' musical evenings, and our host introduced us to him. We could look at him to our hearts' content while he talked to us in a very friendly way. His finely chiselled features and the distinction and kindness of his face are deeply engraved on my memory. As we were living near the buildings of the General Staff, we often saw him in the street, usually alone in the Tiergarten. We were grieved that we did not have the same good fortune with regard to Bismarck ; we never saw him, as he rarely showed himself in public at that time.

I made two dear friends : Marion Schwabe, who later married a grandson of Carl Maria von Weber ; and Mary Meyer, daughter of the Direktor of the National Galleries, who married the art historian Dr. Konrad Fiedler, after whose death she became the wife of her first love and our old friend, Hermann Levi.

Our mother continued to give us every opportunity of making progress in music. She was always ready to give us lessons, arranged ensemble playing with violinists and 'cellists for us, and encouraged us in the study of harmony, for which we could not have found a better master than our uncle Bargiel. I met with the same experience as before. One day Marie and I did not agree about a chord of—I believe—an augmented sixth, and as usual we laid our difficulty before our mother. ' On which degree is this chord built ? ' we asked. ' On which degree ? ' she said. ' I don't know, but you can modulate from it either like this or like this.' And she played some exquisite modulations into four different keys. Marie and I looked at each other in silence. What poor things we were ! What did our small knowledge and ambitions amount to compared with her heaven-sent gift ? Marie courageously persevered, but I told my uncle once and for all that his efforts were wasted on me.

I had a small but, as Stockhausen said, sympathetic voice, and a great wish to sing. Mamma at once consented to my taking lessons. When I had studied for a time with a lady professor at the College of Music, I passed on to Stockhausen. He took a great deal of trouble with me, but as I was often ill I did not do him much credit. I have, however, been grateful all my life that he gave me an insight into the technique of singing, as this became very useful to me later on.

Considering all these advantages our life in Berlin had very pleasant sides, and we ought to have been happy there. Yet such was not the case, although we could hardly have given cogent reasons for this. We did not like Berlin. Perhaps we took an unreasonable dislike to it because our mother was attacked by severe neuritis in her arm during the first year. It was heart-breaking to see her, who had always been so active, condemned not only to complete inactivity but also to incessant pain. This went on not for weeks only but for fully eighteen months. As usual when trouble had to be met, she strove with all her soul to bear the inevitable with patience and not grieve us more than could be helped. She sought consolation and distraction in the interests of others. And how much help she was able to give ! An untold number of young musicians were always applying to her for advice and help : pianists, music teachers, composers who sent their compositions. She found publishers for many early works, posts for many talented young musicians. And how delighted she was when success attended her efforts, how unwilling to discourage those who were without talent ! Yet she did not shirk the duty of persuading these to take up some other career. Though she was not anxious at that time to extend her activity as a teacher, she took a few talented pupils. One of them, Fräulein Mathilde Wendt, soon became a friend of hers and of ours also. Her love and enthusiasm for my mother kept her and her lifelong companion and friend, Fräulein Jungius, in constant touch with us after we left Berlin. Now she is one of the few who still share our memories of great times and hold to the ideals left to us.

Of course, our mother's interest was not limited to musicians. On the contrary, she cast her nets far and wide, and, however modest the place which the acquaintance could claim, my mother's kindness was never failing. Many little affairs of the heart gave rise to her being teased by her daughters. There was the hefty, rosy masseuse, with her fat arms bare to the elbows, who came in the mornings to massage Mamma's arm. We did not grudge her the high fee, nor the bottle of beer and the sandwiches which she demanded as refreshment in the course of an hour's treatment, nor her incessant chatter, for Mamma always listened with great attention. But we did object to her complaining that her work was so exhausting. With this she massaged our mother's tender heart until we found her in tears of compassion. The climax of the episode was reached when the lady told our mother that she too belonged to the artist world of Berlin, as her son was engaged at the Imperial Opera House. Mamma came to dinner quite full of this intelligence ; we were sceptical. Steffen ? We could not remember ever to have seen the name in any programme. We begged her to find out what parts the son was taking, and she told us next day, half amused, half embarrassed, that he was playing third lobster in the ballet ' Flick and Flock.'

In the beginning of 1874 Mamma went to Kiel with Marie, where she sought and found cure for her trouble under Professor Esmarch's treatment. I remained in Berlin, and gained, during these months of separation from my own family, a lasting happiness in the friendship of a young concert singer. She was a Viennese, had studied at the Conservatoire under Mme. Mathilde Marchesi, and came to Germany with recommendations from Brahms, who had advised her to continue her studies and start her career there. First she went to Leipzig and introduced herself to the Herzogenbergs. These delightful people received her with the greatest hospitality, first as a visitor, then as a member of their household. She then came to Berlin, where my mother also received her with great kindness. I soon became intimate with her, and our friendship has been one for life. She was different from all the friends I had made so far. She had a great sense of humour, was so quick at repartee that there was ' go ' in every party when she was present, had the true Austrian good-natured, easy-going temperament, never took life too seriously, rather took hold of it with both hands and made herself at home everywhere. Always faithful to herself, she did not care what any one thought of her, was proof against influences foreign to her nature, and refused to have anything to do with North German ways and manners. Such was Marie Fillunger, or ' Fillu ' as I called her to avoid mistakes about the two Maries. And Fillu she has been to every one since. When Mamma was once asked by a friend to call her by her Christian name and refused, she was reminded, ' But there are others whom you call by their Christian names.' ' Well, yes, there is Fillu, it 's true,' Mamma said. Once when Fillu was walking along Unter den Linden, a cab drew up at the kerb and Joachim called out loudly, ' Fillu, Fillu, do you want a lift ? ' That was too much even for good-natured Fillu, for after the Franco-German war ' filou ' meant every kind of scamp in Germany. Fillu was small, with brown hair and intelligent, kind brown eyes, a mouth which was both sensitive and obstinate, tiny hands and feet. Her speaking voice was a deep alto, her singing voice a most glorious soprano. Joachim once said that it was one of the rare voices which had sensuous charm. I thought so too ; I have never heard another voice with equal charm. It was always there ; even when Fillu had not sung a note for weeks it needed no practising, but issued smooth and mellow from her throat. With incomparable ease she took soprano parts like those in the Ninth Symphony or the ' Peri ' ; her tone remained full and round in the extreme notes of her compass. Only lately I was told that Marie Fillunger had never been equalled since in these parts in Germany.

Yet hers was not an easy life, and we shared difficult times together. But she never lost her courage or her cheerfulness, and in addition helped me when times of depression came over me. I blessed my mother for the kindness with which she accepted my friend, for the help she gave her, as though she had been one of us. She entered into all our difficulties, eased them where she could, exerted her influence in the musical world on Fillu's behalf, and was glad of every engagement. But above all she helped Fillu musically. She rehearsed my father's songs, his ' Peri,' and other things with her when she was singing them in public ; giving special attention to clear enunciation and diction. I greatly enjoyed accompanying Fillu, and learnt a great deal through daily practising with her.

My new friend brought me into closer contact with Heinrich and Liesl von Herzogenberg. My heart warms at the remembrance of them. What an ideal couple they were ! Both young at that time, highly cultured, and imbued with great ideals. When I met Liesl for the first time she wore a red velvet dress ; a mass of wavy golden hair set off the exquisite delicacy of her complexion and her features ; her eyes, golden with a tinge of green, had a most winning expression. I fancied I saw a lady in a picture of the Italian Renaissance. There was something of a charming boyishness in the simplicity and vivacity of her nature. Heinrich, tall and thin, with his aristocratic reserve and monotonous nasal voice, seemed at first sight a curious contrast ; but, knowing him better, one soon saw that these two were made for each other, that each could have found a complement and supreme happiness only in the other. Music was the centre round which their existence turned. Heinrich was a composer who worked indefatigably ; and Liesl, although she was not a composer, was his equal in musical knowledge, for her eminent talent had been early recognised and carefully trained. She had a sensitive, mobile mind, and receptive faculty to a quite unusual degree. And this same Liesl, who was capable of writing down from memory a movement of a new Brahms' symphony after hearing it once, was capable also of turning out a perfect dinner with her own hands. Like the daughters of the Viennese aristocracy, she, the Hanoverian Ambassador's daughter, had learnt cooking under a *chef* in the household of one of the Archdukes ; and I remember her opening the door to me one day when I had just got to know her, with a spoon and a basin in her hand, and in a white overall which was most becoming to her fair type of beauty.

They lived together like two children who, unrestrained by conventions and prejudices, fully enjoy the moment. When we were absorbed in music nobody thought of meals. Both were extraordinarily indifferent to material comforts. Coming home from a concert one evening we found the table laid for supper, but apparently nothing to eat, when our hostess's clear voice called to the kitchen for fried eggs, one by one, until we had all had as many as we wanted. There was something spontaneous and personal, also, in the taste displayed in their home : the charmingly artistic or curiously interesting objects had evidently been acquired without reference to each other, just because each had pleased them. Their taste was the least little bit eccentric, and they were nicknamed ' the Japanese ' on that account by an artist friend of theirs.

The Herzogenbergs had means enough to make their

lives very comfortable, but their generosity was so touchingly great that they needed much, very much, for others. What they had done for Fillu when they took her away from a wretched boarding-house to be their guest, they did for many others, and they did more than that. They were quite incapable of refusing any one who needed or asked for their help. Once an aunt had left them a little money, and whenever an opportunity arose they decided, 'We will nibble the aunt.' In the end they were still nibbling her when she had long been consumed.

My mother was very fond of Liesl, whose musical gifts and thorough understanding were a great joy to her. What Liesl felt for my mother is beautifully expressed in a letter written to me in 1887 : ' It has been a refreshment to my heart to have seen your mother again, though her visit was far too short. I am not given to many words where I feel most, but I had to tell her openly how deeply I am devoted to her ; what riches, what happiness, knowing her and being a little beloved by her has brought into my life. Whenever I think of her face bathed in sunshine, something inexpressible comes over me. She is growing more and more beautiful, too, this dear mother ; her artist's soul, her childlike purity, her motherly goodness, shine forth more and more gloriously from her wonderful eyes. It is a joy to look at her.'

Liesl had no children, alas ! How delightful it would have been to see a number of little Heinrichs and Liesls grow up ! It was a sorrow to her which only her sunny disposition, her love for Heinrich, and her eager interest in outside pursuits helped her to forget. In every other way Providence seemed to have so favoured these two that it seemed doubly cruel when bitter experiences and sickness overclouded their lives and cut them prematurely short. Their pretty home in the Bavarian mountains, the ' Lieselei,' on which they had stamped their charm and goodness, had to be given up, and it was hoped that

Liesl might be cured by the higher air of the Appenzell mountains. But she never reached her new home ; Heinrich buried her in a foreign land, and, mortally ill himself, lived alone where he had hoped to dwell with her. ' Afterglow,' he called the house where he lingered expectant of the morning glow of reunion. Their fate was a great grief to the whole circle which had gathered round my mother, Brahms, and Joachim, and of which they had been one of the brightest ornaments. Heinrich and Liesl were of those who take much of the joy and glory of this earth with them when they leave us.

When we moved to Frankfurt in 1878, Fillu went with us. Mamma and Marie had already left Berlin, while Fillu and I saw to the packing up. So it happened that we were still there on the second of June, the terrible day of Nobiling's attempt on the life of the Emperor William the First. All hearts beat in unison in their fear and sympathy for the venerable monarch, in horror at the deed. No other thought was possible ; people could not rest within their four walls ; every human being was out in the streets in hopes of hearing news. Fillu and I were no exception to the rule ; we were soon among an enormous crowd which, tightly packed, was moving slowly towards the Imperial residence, where it halted. We looked round, so far as that was possible. There they were, as far as the eye could reach—a sea of human faces ! Not only the square but also the adjoining streets were packed. In perfect silence, so as not to disturb the Imperial patient, we all stood ; every eye was riveted upon the window at which it had been usual of late years to see the Emperor show himself. Now and then some one appeared at this window and looked silently upon the anxious watchers below. Suddenly a breath of relief spread from the front ranks. Who can teil what first gave rise to it ? But we all knew : the doctors had given hope, the Emperor was expected to recover. The news spread like a conflagration through

the masses, almost without a word. As though relieved
from a nightmare, the crowd began to move ; it surged
back as it had come, slowly gliding, dissolving. Fillu
and I, we hardly knew how, found ourselves back in the
quietude of Unter den Zelten.

The person of the Emperor had been dear and familiar
to me since the days of my childhood, when we watched
him on the Promenade at Baden while we were at breakfast in our cosy arbour, and from later years, when I had
seen him riding in the Tiergarten or driving along Unter
den Linden. But since the year 1876 I had a particularly tender feeling for him, for I believed, and still
believe, that I was the centre of interest for him once for
a few moments. It was in Ems, where I was taking the
waters. I was on my obligatory early walk one morning
in a lonely part of the park, when I saw the Emperor
coming towards me with some gentlemen. I was almost
paralysed, but there was no way of escape, I was obliged
to pass him. He drew nearer—I stood aside—the
moment came, and I curtsied deeply. My eyes were
riveted on his face. He acknowledged my curtsy with
a chivalrous, fatherly, truly royal salute. During the
single moment when his eyes rested on me he seemed to
read me through and through. I felt distinctly that he
thought of nothing at that moment but this one small
subject of his ; to me he belonged for the time being,
and never have I forgotten that look. I have only found
it in persons of outstanding qualities who, with full
realisation of all their powers, can give themselves up
entirely to the impressions of the moment.

II

A new life began for us in Frankfurt. My mother's
professional activities were the centre of our interests,
especially as Marie and I were soon appointed as her
assistants.

It was a privilege to work for and with her, to apply what we had learnt from her, to be guided by her advice, and to be able to refer to her as the highest authority. How glad she was when we were successful, how unwilling to take our good pupils from us when they were far enough advanced to enter her classes ! Yet this was our ambition and our pride.

The earnestness and devotion which my mother brought to all her work made itself felt once more in her teaching. She was not contented only with giving the appointed time and professional training to each pupil, but studied their individualities in all their requirements, knowing that these must be taken into account in the making of good musicians and performers. She knew that a hard-working young student must be well nourished, properly guided and advised during the years of adolescence, and that general culture was indispensable for every artist. And, assisted by Marie, she took charge of all this when parents of the pupils were for some reason unable to do so. A number of generous Frankfurt citizens, whose interest had been secured, supplied her with the means, which they raised by subscription. She was at liberty to dispose of them to young talented students as she thought best. This added considerably to her work, but it was a labour of love which was repaid by the joy of being able to help. It would have been much more difficult in Berlin to enlist a similar general interest in the music students. In this as in other ways we felt the advantage of living in one of the smaller towns ; Frankfurt could still be regarded as one of these at that time. The North German element, added since 1866, was kept entirely outside the inner circle of old-established Frankfurt families, who were still sore against Prussia. Others took up a half-conciliatory attitude. Society was divided into coteries, which admitted outsiders with the consent of all their members only. The advantage of this was that one met the same people over and over again and got to know them really well. We took a great interest in each other, and became more intimate than the members of larger and looser circles in large towns could ever be. Life was more cheerful, more easy-going, owing to the general prosperity. Every one had ample means, and did not grudge his neighbour what was his. With just pride the Frankfurters boasted that there were no poor in the town. In spite of their wealth, people could be said to live simply; there was no vulgar display, such as had often disagreeably impressed us in Berlin.

We were welcomed kindly, I may say affectionately, and soon felt at home. The greater restriction in the social life did not make it less interesting. Individualities had more chance of developing; the feminine element especially, as represented by the hostesses of our circle, who were nicknamed ' the Great Wives,' showed such pronounced types in so great a variety that dullness could not thrive where they were. Some incident or other was sure to keep our attention fixed, our interest or our humour alive.

It was a great additional pleasure that our sister Elise and her husband, Herr Sommerhoff, also came to live in Frankfurt; that we could share in her happiness and see her charming children grow up. A beloved old friend, Marie Berna, now Countess Oriola, was living on her large property at Büdesheim, not far from the town, and we spent many delightful hours in her beautiful home.

The Stockhausens, too, had settled in Frankfurt, and were living so near that we could see a great deal of each other. I was now enabled to appreciate him fully as a musician and personally. So far I had more or less taken him for granted as a wonderful singer and a great friend of my mother's. I saw how music was his element, almost to the exclusion of everything else. His enthusiasm was irresistible, and occasionally made him break down conventional barriers. I remember a concert in Berlin, where he was conductor of Dr. Stern's Choral Society, when they performed Brahms's 'Song of Destiny' for the first time. He had rehearsed it with the infinite care which he bestowed on all his work. The last chords had died down and the audience began to applaud. Stockhausen turned round, his face aglow with emotion. 'Ladies and gentlemen,' he said, 'I am sure I shall only carry out your wishes if I give you an opportunity of hearing this wonderful work again at once.'

Strange that it was Stockhausen, of foreign origin on his mother's side, who with the fiery, restless temperament inherited from her should have made the Germans fully aware of the glorious treasure which they possessed in their songs. His singing of the Müllerlieder, Dichter-liebe, 'Faust,' has never been equalled.

Not long after us the Landgravine of Hesse also settled in Frankfurt. She and my mother had been friends for many years. The distinguished Hohenzollern Princess, a niece of the Emperor William the First, had had my devoted admiration from my childhood, and now, after a lifetime, I still gratefully remember her many kind-nesses to us. It sometimes happens that words are little heeded at the moment when they are spoken, but remain at the back of one's mind and are remembered when the time comes to take them to heart. This is what happened to me when the Princess said, 'Eugenie, why do you write in Latin characters? You are a German, and should use our German characters.' I paid no attention to this admonition, and continued to write in Latin characters, because they are less tiring for the hand. But the time came when I recognised that to use them was a symbol of loyalty, and that a German woman had wished to impress this upon me at the time. I spent many hours with her eldest daughter, the charm-ing Princess Elisabeth, later Hereditary Princess of Anhalt. Though she was several years younger than I,

JULIUS STOCKHAUSEN

we had many interests in common ; she appreciated music sincerely and with understanding.

When my memory carries me back to the Frankfurt days, faces of friends without number pass before me. Could I but name them all, tell in words what they have been to us ! All our old friends came to see us. Brahms from Vienna, Levi from Munich, the Herzogenbergs from Leipzig, the Volklands from Basle. Dear Frau Kufferath, who had preserved the freshness of youth throughout a long life which had not always been easy, who liked to tease and let herself be teased, came from Brussels and brought her youngest daughter Antonia, with her sphinx-like eyes and a voice of unusually beautiful quality, who became engaged to Mr. Speyer at our house. My mother's friend, Friedchen Sauermann, came from Hamburg ; she was well known in musical circles of the time under her maiden name of Friedchen Wagner, had been a pupil of Brahms in his early Hamburg days, and the leading singer in his Choir for Women's Voices. It was he who had at that time introduced her to my mother. She was small and plain, of passionate temperament and high spirits, showed her love so truly and her hatred— in which she would indulge occasionally in spite of her sincere piety—so delightfully ! She was devoted to our mother, and kept her memory enshrined in her heart as her most precious possession.

My mother's old girl-friends came, foremost among them *Emilie List* from Munich, daughter of the famous economist, Friedrich List ; the ' girl with a spirit of fire,' as my father had called her. She was very intellectual, a passionate politician, and enthusiastically patriotic. Spirit of fire still dwelt in her eyes, which were large and rather protruding. The youthful friend she had remained in every sense of the word ; she cherished every tie that was between her and our mother, and took up the threads again after years of separation. We were always glad when she came, for her presence had a most stimulating effect on our mother. She was the most intimate of all her friends ; occasionally they could be like girls together. I remember their coming home after a walk, telling us with great delight that they had lost their way in the fields behind the Grüneberg, and had been obliged to climb the gates to get out. Emilie laughed at Klara, Klara at Emilie. No wonder ! Who would not have been amused to see these two tall and portly old ladies, both in their seventieth year, perform this acrobatic feat ? We could not think how they had managed to do it.

Now and then Frau *Emma Preusser* came, an old lady with silvery little curls under a black lace cap, her features so delicate, her figure so dainty, and in whom a truly Christian spirit dwelt. She had had many trials, which she bore with admirable resignation, even serenity. While Emilie List had been a witness, and indeed an agent herself, in my mother's romantic love story, the friendship with Frau Emma Preusser had begun during the time when my parents lived in Dresden.

Then there was *Livia Frege*, the Leipzig patrician's wife, somewhat distant and imposing, whose musical gifts and interests had early drawn her and my mother together. She had been a concert singer before her marriage, and created the title part in my father's ' Peri.'

Pauline Viardot, too, once more visited us ; she was quite unchanged, seemed as young and full of the joy of life as ever, still kissed the air while she cried, ' Mein Klärchen ! mein Klärchen ! ' and was unalterably loyal and affectionate.

Many of the new acquaintances who played a part in our lives in the 'eighties were only transitory ; others took permanent places. Foremost among these were Karl and Loucky von der Mühll Burckhardt in Basle, whose acquaintance I also owed to Fillu. Loucky became a sister to me, Karl a faithful friend. Both loved and admired my mother and were beloved by her. They were an entirely new type to me, and the atmosphere of their home differed from anything I had yet known. There never had been placid times in my life; I cannot remember any periods of quiet, contemplative existence. Our mother's profession and her position in the world entailed perpetual demands from outside. She herself never lost the sense of balance, of repose; she held straight on her course amid the high tide of life. Hers was a wonderfully strong character, made perfect in joy and sorrow by strict adherence to duty, and moreover finding a sure haven of rest in music. I, on the other hand, sharing my mother's life and wrestling with my own ambitions and difficulties as well, often found it hard to keep my head above water. I remember how I suffered after my sister Julie's death when no time, however short, was given me to indulge in my grief. On other occasions also the crude contrast between our inner and our outer life came home to me and often put me out of harmony with myself. Here at last was a home in which peace and quietness reigned for ever, and this home opened its doors to me in friendship. Would that I could paint the house and its inmates in words of beautiful colours ! Loucky, gracious, sunny, glad of life, with a warm, open mind ; Karl, shy and ashamed of his good soft heart, tried to hide it behind assumed roughness.

Long ago I knew a child of twelve, strong and healthy, with rosy cheeks and curved lips. She was sitting on the window-sill with her back towards the room, dangling her legs outside, gazing at nothing. Every one in the room was busy with something or other. I yielded to an impulse to tease the child. ' Elsie,' I said, ' look, every one is busy, and you, young and strong, are doing nothing.' The child threw back her head with a proud movement and said loudly and firmly, ' I ? I am living.' What I had then with astonishment and emotion learnt for the first time from the lips of a child, I found again in perfection in the home in Auf dem Gellert.

Karl and Loucky were content to 'be living.' They were living a life which held neither self-consciousness nor ambitions, but the impulses of which were 'helpful, noble, and good.' They had no struggles or difficulties. Rare differences of opinion between them were settled peacefully and almost without words ; this seemed all the more wonderful to me because both were of a vivacious temperament. One gave way to the other in silence ; neither hampered the inclinations of the other, but affectionately encouraged them. As Loucky had no children, Karl was glad that she should have friends to whom she could give her affection, and accepted them as part of their lives. During thirty-five years, when I frequently, and often for months, stayed with these friends, I always found the same peace and harmony. Even when trouble in the shape of Karl's long invalidism found them out, it was not allowed to take peace away from their home. When I was far from them, the mere idea that this sunlit home existed was a consolation to me. I knew that whatever storms were passing outside, life within went at its accustomed pace. Karl would be sitting at the window at a certain time reading his newspaper, or at the table rolling cigarettes or playing patience. Again, he would put on his fireman's uniform and attend the practices ; or perform his honorary duties in various quarters of the town, to-day at an orphanage, to-morrow at a Friendly Society. Loucky, who was never unoccupied, although she always seemed to have leisure, would see to everything in house and garden, look after the chickens, incite Kikerle, her faithful little King Charles, to run after the cat when cries of frightened birds proclaimed its proximity. Whenever any wounded thing came her way—and somehow they constantly did —she would bind up wounds, soothe, and comfort.

I was most hospitably received, also, in the large circle of Loucky's brothers and sisters, who were living on their own four properties in Auf dem Gellert in true unity and love. Although temperamentally different from each other, they were alike in that distinction which in old-established families is due partly to tradition, partly to culture. All were eminently endowed with artistic gifts, with which they adorned their daily lives, without further ambition.

Our domestic life in Frankfurt was as regular as it had been elsewhere. Breakfast was the most leisurely meal ; Mamma read her letters—rather, she read them to us. As long as I can remember she never received a letter which she did not communicate to us, although she did not expect the same in return. She was, however, always pleased when we did so of our own free will. Afterwards she wrote letters, played a little, and began her lessons at half-past ten. When the lessons were over she either went for a walk or for a drive, when her pupils would be the subject of conversation between us. After dinner she rested, and allowed herself a harmless little relaxation in which she had never before indulged. She read the serial stories in the newspaper, and they would often make her so excited that she told us each day what had happened to the characters. When she was away, we always carefully kept the numbers for her, and on her return she acknowledged our attention with an affectionate smile. From four to five she again played, and then received her many visitors at tea-time. When they had left and we were alone once more, Mamma again sat down at her writing-table. I would then some-times kneel down by her, and she talked to me of her troubles, for she was never without them. She often thought of death and separation from us, and I comforted her as best I could, promising that it should not be long before I joined her, when she would look at me with inexpressible tenderness and caress my cheek, and I felt that I had lightened her heart a little.

In earlier days Mamma often read to us in the evenings : studies by Stifter, short stories by Otto Ludwig, Arnim's

Guardians of the Crown, biographical works and memoirs, essays by Treitschke, Konrad Ferdinand Meyer's and Gottfried Keller's novels, etc. Later she took to playing whist, and her little rubber after the day's activities became a pleasant habit. I greatly admired her for giving it up from the moment when her grandson Ferdinand came to live with us. She thought it important that he should acquire general culture as well as his musical education, and we read *Wilhelm Meister* in the evenings. She made Ferdinand read, so that he should get practice in this also. The sacrifice of a small daily habit would have come very hardly to me, but my mother made it as a matter of course.

We often begged Mamma in the evenings to tell us of her youth. She would always begin with our grandfather and tell us how he had given all his best efforts to her in preference to her brothers and sisters ; how he had spoilt her in spite of his severity, given the best bits to her at meal-times. She said that she owed her excellent health to his insistence on regularity in everything. He had imparted his love of work and strict sense of duty to her, and her mother that of order in small things.

What she had minded more than anything else had been her father's boasting of her gifts ; she had also felt quite early that it was inartistic to improvise in public or play a Chopin Study transposed merely for display. Her father had even insisted on her doing it when she played to Chopin.

We never tired of hearing about her early devotion to our father, at the age of thirteen, when she had been so unhappy to hear of his engagement to Ernestine von Fricken. We used to say, ' Oh, if we could only have known you then ! ' but she assured us she had been very plain at that time. This we did not believe. One after another, famous pianists whom she had known and other artists would be described to us. She had had the greatest admiration for Liszt's genius, for the irresistible fire and *élan* of his playing, but his influence on composers and young pianists she considered fatal. He had always been most courteous and chivalrous to her. When they were in Vienna at the same time in 1838, and he drove her home in his carriage after a musical party, she was out of spirits because people had talked incessantly during her playing. She complained of it to Liszt, and he said, ' Yes, on these occasions you should play some rotten thing by Liszt.'

Our mother always spoke with the greatest delight of Mendelssohn ; his legato, his playing altogether, she said, were perfect. But no other pianist's touch had so discouraged her as Adolf Henselt's ; she had never hoped to reach such beauty and perfection, and had cried for days after hearing him. Felix Mendelssohn was the musician who appealed most to her as a human being, she had loved him truly ; the remembrance of him could still bring a light into her eyes. She extended her affection to his children and to all who were connected with him.

Of the women musicians it was Wilhelmine Schröder-Devrient whom she loved most. Whenever she thought of this wonderful artist and of her fate, who with her fiery temperament and passionate heart had been pre-destined to love and to suffer, she was overcome with emotion.

She sometimes spoke of our father, of his indescribably beautiful improvisations, and then I became indescribably sad never to have heard them. ' They were as beautiful as his known compositions, so perfect in form that, had they been taken down, they could have been published without alteration.'

She told us how unassuming he had been, how indifferent to success at the moment, and yet how conscious of his worth. When she had been depressed sometimes because his works were not making headway with the public fast enough, he would say, ' Never mind, in ten years' time it will be quite different.'

While she talked, the forms of those long gone and of others whom I myself had still known passed before my inner vision. How great, how distinguished they were, holding on their course like the stars without clashing ! They all were human, had their faults and weaknesses, but they were great in placing their art higher than themselves. I am thinking among others of the young Joachim. He had given rise to great hopes as a creative artist; some had placed him above Brahms. But as soon as he had realised Brahms's greater genius he yielded his place most beautifully and generously. He devoted his energy to the interpretation of his friend's works, and opened the hearts of his contemporaries to receive them. He can hardly have given up his own ambitions without a struggle, and others may have had similar experiences. But they were all united in the love for high ideals, working gladly and harmoniously together. Truly, it was a great time !

AN ATTEMPT

FAMILIAR to us from our earliest childhood, yet fresh every day, our mother's art ever remained a wonder to us. In comparison to this everything seemed insignificant ; it stood in the forefront of our lives. In her art as well as in herself my mother was daily a new experience to me, not merely because my understanding of music was steadily maturing, but because she whom I had known from a child as an artist of the highest rank never stood still, but fixed her aim ever higher. For instance, I remember her playing to me Brahms's Fantasia, op. 116, and the Intermezzo in C sharp minor, op. 117, when they had just been published. She played them wonderfully, so that they haunted me for months. I went to England, and when I returned after three months I begged her to play them to me again. She did, but how she played them ! I exclaimed in amazement, ' Mamma, what progress you have made ! How is it possible ? ' What was the difference ? I can hardly explain it. They had been wonderful works of art before, but they had now become spiritualised, transfigured. No longer single beauties stood out. They had become plastic creations, glowing with life and tenderness. Another time I asked her to play me the first bars of the accompaniment of ' Schöne Fremde ' from the (Schumann) Eichendorf Liederkreis, in which I was often accompanying Fillu. I had been studying hard and felt that I had made progress and had come a little nearer my mother's standard. Mamma sat down and played. Tears of emotion poured from my eyes ; from that moment I buried every hope of reaching my ideal.

How the legato of the melody hovered above that of the bass, while the semiquavers subordinated themselves severely to the rhythmic design and yet displayed a beauty of their own ! How these three, melody, bass, and semiquavers, were blended in perfect poetry, equal to that of poet and composer ! Yes, that touch was unattainable !

'TO FRAU KLARA SCHUMANN,
THE GREATEST SINGER.'

With this inscription Brahms as a youth had dedicated to her a copy of his second opus of songs, sent from Hamburg in November 1854. Nothing truer or more apposite has been said of her touch, which conveyed like a beautiful human voice every shade of emotion. Her faultless legato gave soul to the melody, carrying-power to her piano, and that extraordinary strength to brilliant passages of which Goethe had said as early as 1831, ' The girl has more power than six boys.'

Mamma herself used to say that she never felt her fingers while she was playing, and this, I think, is characteristic. I could never have thought of fingers when I heard her, and I have never heard any comments on her technique. To whom would technical difficulties have occurred on hearing the enormous climaxes in ' Marche des Davidsbündler contre les Philistins,' or in the second movement of the Fantasia, op. 17, or the last movement of the F sharp minor Sonata? And yet, if the composer's intentions with regard to crescendo and presto are carried out exactly, these movements present almost insuperable difficulties. Why was it that my mother's interpretation never suggested these? Undoubtedly because her technique was made entirely subservient to the musical thought and feeling. As a means to an end her technique was perfect and infallible. It sounds almost incredible, and yet it is true that I have never known my mother to fail in the most difficult passages, such as the end of the second movement of the Fantasia, op. 17, where the demand on the player is truly enormous if full value is given to the semiquavers, yet at the same time full play to the utmost passion. We children knew that this required all her physical strength, but the audience never guessed it, and even I would forget it in the overwhelmingly emotional effect of her playing.

I once admired her shake, and she told me that she had bestowed special care upon it after a critic had found fault with it. 'You know,' she said, 'that as a rule I do not take much notice of newspaper criticism, but this observation struck me, and after due reflection I came to the conclusion that the man was right. My father had never made me practise the shake in particular, but I now made it my special study until there was no fault to be found with it.'

But even this now perfect shake was subordinated to the musical thought ; it remained a means to an end, and its character changed with the character of the piece. The chain of trills in Chopin's Notturno in B major ; the shakes and runs in Brahms's Romance in F major, op. 118, which are in the nature of accompanying instruments ; the little introductory trill of the Gluck Gavotte set by Brahms ' for Frau Klara Schumann ' ; the point-d'orgue shake in the sixth variation of the Beethoven Sonata, op. 119, in E major—who would have thought of technical perfection and a beautiful shake when listening to them ? Melancholy trembled in the long-drawn, gentle plaint of the trill in the Notturno ; in Brahms's Romance the imagination was charmed with pictures of shepherd boys playing their reeds while the brook plashes over the pebbles and summer peace reigns all around. A daring little intruder to whom one gladly accorded a smile of welcome, the trill of the Gluck Gavotte leaped into the strict rhythm of the melody. I and a few others knew how this effect was produced and how difficult it was, for my mother did not play a short trill but one of several beats in which the accent was given on the principal note ; she thereby preserved the strict rhythm of the melody. But even knowing this I never could understand where she took the time from, so as never apparently to shorten either the preceding or the principal note. In the Beethoven Sonata, whose soul would not have been deeply stirred by the titanic climax which my mother produced by means of the point-d'orgue shake ? It swelled like a storm, threatening a cataclysm, but led back in a marvellous diminuendo to the heavenly peace of the theme. Here, too, those who understood knew but forgot what technical mastery was required to make the musical thought triumph. I was present when a Berlin public in 1878 broke into a frenzy of enthusiasm at the end of this sonata and did not rest until my mother consented to repeat the last movement.

I felt towards my mother's playing as towards a monument of Gothic art, where the strict symmetry of all the lines which tend upward to the highest point seems ever new to the eye, however often we may have looked upon it. She built up every piece of music grandly, passionately, logically. There was no hurry, no sudden climax ; conforming to strict artistic laws, yet apparently spontaneous and free, each creation flowed from the hands of the artist, holding the listener in thrall to the end.

Those who have heard her play the Beethoven Concertos, my father's in A minor, Chopin's in F minor, or Mozart's in D minor, will agree with me that they are indelibly engraved on the soul ; no one else's rendering could erase hers. Certain things, such as Beethoven's Eroica Variations, I have only heard my mother play once, but have retained them exactly as she played them.

It may easily be imagined how precious was the instruction which I gathered from her in the course of so many years, and how carefully I have preserved it. When I played Beethoven's ' Moonlight ' Sonata for the first time, I took the Allegretto very fast. ' That won't do,' said my mother ; ' that is far too quick ; the Allegretto character is completely lost.' I said that I felt it quick, and she replied, ' You must feel this movement in its relation to the two other movements. It is a bridge between the Adagio sostenuto and the Presto agitato ; if you play it too fast, the contrast with the first movement is too great.' I then tried it slower, but that took all the life out of it. My mother proposed that I should lay the sonata aside till I was more mature and could feel it differently. A few years later, when I took it up again, the right tempo came quite naturally to me.

When I studied Beethoven's Sonata in C major, op. 53, with her, she said, ' Pupils often bring me editions with arbitrary dynamic notation by the editors. One of them has marked the second theme of the first movement slower by the metronome. I consider this wrong. If you were to check me by the metronome, you would probably find that I was actually playing the second theme more slowly. This is an integral part of the character of both themes, but it must not sound as if the tempo had been changed intentionally. The player as well as the listener must feel that a gradual quieting down of the preceding bars has naturally prepared the slower tempo, and that the flow of the composition has not been broken. The same rule applies where you return to the quicker tempo of the first theme. The player should always graduate, not cut up ; concentrate, not diffuse. Beethoven has been careful to mark changes of tempo where he wished for them.'

She could not impress strongly enough upon me how careful one should be with changes of tempo in my father's music. They ought always to conform to the character of the piece. A ritardando should never be played where it was not marked, never be extended beyond the notes actually so marked. The very short ritardandi are, she said, more in the nature of an emphasis on the few notes, like that of Chopin's short sostenuto.

I often realised how right my mother was when I heard others play my father's music. In the last movement of the G minor Sonata, for instance, the second theme, which is marked ' a little slower,' is sometimes played at half the time of the Presto. Apart from its being contrary to the composer's intention, the arbitrary change of tempo simply kills the whole movement. I not only felt this myself, but could observe the same effect on the audience. These fanciful changes of mood in my father's works demand all the more to be bound together by a dominating tempo. This of course implies a high degree of creative faculty, which was so striking a feature of my mother's playing. The Romance in B major, op. 28, comes into my mind. We and our friends have heard her play it many times, and always it attracted, charmed, even surprised us anew. The loveliness of the melody, the charming tossing to and fro in the first Intermezzo, the melancholy sweetness of the second, would sufficiently explain this. Yet I believe it to have been the strict rhythm of the first period which made this Romance so great a work of art. My mother played this first period, which is repeated four times in the course of the piece, each time in exactly the same tempo to a hair's-breadth. By this means she created a firm basis on which free play could be given to her fancy without loss of the sense of unity in the composition. But how exact must be a sense of rhythm which returns to a tempo four times with minutest exactitude where the composer demands seven abrupt changes !

Rhythm is truly described as the soul of music, and in it perhaps the soul of my mother's playing was to be found. What else but her rhythm in the Chopin Study in G flat major, op. 10, would have made a little pupil exclaim in delight, ' Why, it is just like butterflies ! ' If

Photo. Hanfstaengl, Frankfurt a/M.

CLARA SCHUMANN
DURING THE LAST YEARS OF HER LIFE

the brilliance of the passages suggested a feeling of summer, the rhythm beginning at the seventeenth bar, played piano by my mother and in the strict time which the composer intended, might very well have suggested the flight of butterflies from flower to flower, the flutter of their wings, their short, hovering rests.

And it was the perfect balancing of the two rhythms which brought out the incomparable loveliness of the A flat major Valse, op. 42. Again, when I was listening to the Chopin Study in F minor (No. 1 of the posthumous), which flowed from her fingers like a tender dream, I felt I was lying among high, waving grasses, while boughs laden with blossom were softly brushing my forehead. When I asked myself what charm brought this vision before my inward eye, I knew it was the wonderful art with which my mother blended the two rhythms, four quavers in the left and three crotchets in the right hand. Full play was given to the emotions, while she bound herself to strictest rhythm. In perfect independence of each other both hands were joined in heavenly poetry. And yet, the charm of my mother's playing, which remained to the end, cannot be explained by rhythm alone. 'The Unconscious, the Inexplicable : Klara,' Robert Schumann wrote of her in 1831, when she was twelve years old. The intrinsic nature of every art is an eternal mystery, a mystery even to the artist himself.

I started this chapter reluctantly, called it an attempt, and now that I have finished I confess that it was a reckless attempt. I tried to say what cannot be expressed in words, to fix what is fleeting. 'When I am dead, all that I have done will be forgotten ; my art, my aims were in vain,' my mother sometimes said in hours of depression. She went the way of all that is mortal ; the mould into which she poured her soul is broken. But she has not lived in vain. Transformed, her spirit still lives in the influence which she exercised over thousands, and will continue to live from generation to generation.

MEMOIRS OF EUGENIE SCHUMANN

As I wrote these pages I thought of those who have been touched by her spirit. In them my words may awake an echo of what it was, and perhaps convey a glimpse to those who never knew its glory. I dedicate this attempt to the few who still share the remembrance with us.

In Conclusion,

I will reckon up the sum of my experiences and balance light and shade as they fell on my path. Many were the good auguries at our birth, yet life for us children has not been easy. In saying this I do not refer so much to the hard decrees of fate which dealt us blow after blow from our childhood upwards. I am thinking of us as children of parents of genius. Our lives, bound up with theirs, involved certain presuppositions and brought restrictions from the very outset. Although none of us daughters had eminent musical gifts, it was taken for granted that we would choose music as a profession. So far as I was concerned my own musical achievements have satisfied me so little that to me they have been a lifelong martyrdom.

But, on the other hand, the constant occupation with music has enriched and deepened my life as nothing else could have done. Only my attempts enabled me to enter into the nature of my parents' art and to make it my own through understanding. If we had shown distinct gifts or predilections for anything else, this would certainly have been taken into consideration. But the balance was thrown in the direction of music from the first, owing to the strong influences of tradition and the position of the majority of our friends. When I left school, my world was ready-made for me, and I never thought of escaping from it. I was content to love and admire ; and truly, it was one of the greatest privileges of my life that I could give love and admiration to those who were nearest to me, and to many others who combined great artistic or intellectual gifts with high moral qualities.

The world has done us the wrong of judging us too much by comparison with our parents, as human beings as well as musically ; but it made good this injustice by letting us share fully in the love which it bore them, love surviving their death and still revealing itself to us in ways which deeply touch our hearts.

I could say that light and shade had been equally distributed on the path of our lives, if there had not been the one great light which with its brightness gilded even the clouds. This was the light shed by my mother's personality in intimate touch with her. No one on whom the sun of her eyes has shone, who has been wrapped in the warmth of her heart, has lived a life in shadow, but feels deep gratitude towards Providence which revealed itself in divine mother love, thereby implanting in us a belief in love immortal and eternal.

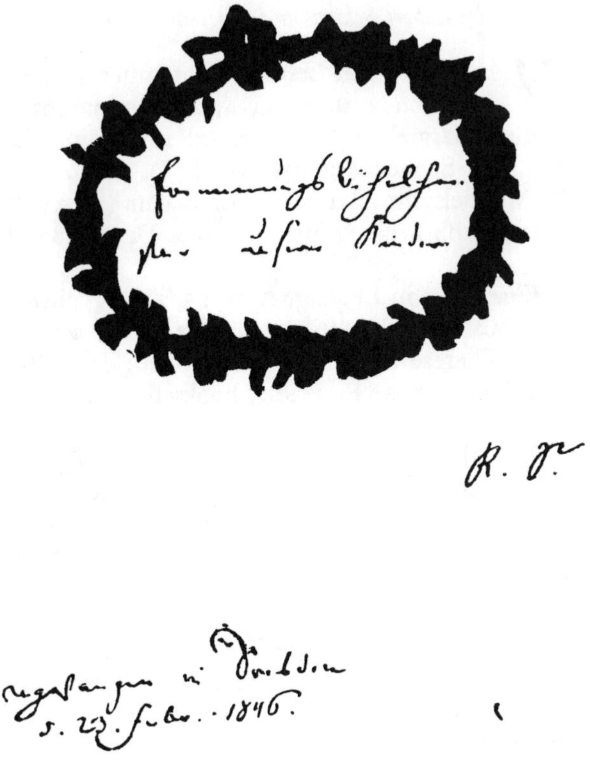
angefangen in Dresden
d. 23. Febr. 1846.

A LITTLE BOOK OF MEMORIES FOR OUR CHILDREN

(*Begun by Robert Schumann in Dresden on February 23, 1846.*)

MARIE, born at Leipzig, September 1, 1841 ; christened on 13th at 11 A.M. Godparents : Grandmother Bargiel (*née* Trommlitz) in Berlin ; Uncle Karl Sch. in Schneeberg (proxy J. A. Barth, publisher) ; F. Mendelssohn Bartholdy in Berlin (proxy R. Härtel, music publisher) ; Mme. Johanna Devrient in Leipzig.

Elise, born in Leipzig, April 25, 1843 ; christened May 6, 9 A.M. Godparents : Auntie Karl, *née* Trommlitz ; Frau Therese Fleischer, *née* Semmel ; Herr Karl Voigt, merchant ; Herr R. Friese, bookseller ; all present.

Julie, born in Dresden, March 11, 1845, at 7 A.M. ; christened April 6. Godparents : Step-grandmamma Wieck, *née* Fechner ; Frau Serre, wife of Major Serre ; Privy Councillor Carus ; Herr Karl Kragen ; all of Dresden.

Emil, born in Dresden, February 8, 1846, 1 P.M. ; christened April 6. Godparents : Frau Livia Frege (wife of Dr. Frege), *née* Gerhardt, from Leipzig ; Professor Eduard Bendemann ; and Conductor Ferdinand Hiller.
He died June 22, 1847.

Ludwig, born in Dresden, January 20, 1848, 1.45 A.M. ; christened March 14. Godparents : Countess Sophie

Baudissin ; Professor J. Hübner ; and the artist R. Reinick.

Marie : Cheerful, vivacious temperament, not very obstinate, responsive to kindness ; pliant, warm-hearted, affectionate. Excellent memory for the smallest events of her little life. Very sensitive to teasing.

Seems fond of music ; no signs of any extraordinary gift. Has begun to knit in February '46 ; seems altogether inclined to be domestic and practical.

Talks a great deal, often incessantly. First sally : Gave her a miniature of her mother, who was in Kopenhagen, to look at, which she licked clean off.

Elise : In many respects the exact opposite of Marie : stubborn, very naughty, often had to feel the birch, greedy. Has very high spirits, more sense of humour than Marie ; thoughtful too, as though reflecting upon things. Spoilt by a doting nurse. When thwarted, struggles with hands and feet.

Marie, on a walk at night, pointing to the evening star : ' Papa, I think the star keeps so near the moon to make her feel less lonely.'

Marie, looking up to the sky after dark on February 22, 1846 : ' Dear God, throw down a few stars for me.'

Almost daily walks with Marie in Dresden, even in bad weather.

Frequently occupy myself in teaching Marie to count, and to look for rhymes.

Marie and Elise often sing with evident pleasure, and have clear, true voices, Elise's specially strong.

Lieschen tells very amusingly the story of the Black Sausage that invites the Liver Sausage to dinner.

On March 26, Marie went to her Grandpapa's by herself for the first time ; she returned very pleased with herself. I am beginning to teach her the keys on the piano.

I have often noticed that children care very little for the beauties of nature (sunsets, storms, etc.).

Julie is developing more slowly than the others ; it may be that she was not given a wet-nurse in good time. At thirteen months she can neither walk nor talk, except to say ' Papa.' On the other hand, music appeals to her very much, she at once begins to sing. An altogether delicate, sensitive little plant.

The children like to be helpful and busy.

Visit to Maxen with Marie and her mother from 10-13 May. Beautifully laid-out gardens, many dogs, good meals. The sheep-pen. Skittles. Beehives.

Helmchen (Hentschel)—Marie's first friend. May 1846.

Herr Bendemann, Herr Hiller, Herr Gade ; Mme. Hiller's present of a beautiful ball.
Names to help Marie to remember : also Herr Mendelssohn and Frau Dr. Frege from Leipzig.

May 25, went with Marie and Elise into the country for a few weeks, to Maxen.
The children's enjoyment. The Major's wife. Herr Kohl. The American swing. Little excursions to the Bush Inn and the Schlottwitz Dell. The butterfly cap. Herr Kragen. Frau von Berge. Miss Margaret.

Marie saying that ' Lieschen had so bedaubed her with chalk that she looked like a white nigger.'

On June 7 Papa found (for the first time in his life) a bird's nest. Therefore patience, dear children. What one has not accomplished in thirty-six years, one may yet accomplish on the last day before entering upon the thirty-seventh, as to my great pleasure I did to-day.

Julchen and Emil with the nurse came out to Maxen later ; all have benefited much by the country air, especially Julchen, who had been constantly ailing, and is very slow in her general development.

On June 28 the children regretfully returned to town.

On July 6 we went to the Isle of Norderney, leaving the children in Dresden under Elwine's care. In our absence Marie and Elise attended Dr. Frankénberg's Kindergarten, where they are very happy.

On August 26 we returned from the seaside, and found the children quite well and happy.

Marie is beginning to learn her letters.

DRESDEN, 29 *March* 1847.

Long journeys and great events have occurred in your lives, especially Marie's and Lieschen's, since my last entry.

September and October were spent quietly and much as usual in Dresden. I went for walks with Marie, often long walks ; she sometimes complains that she is ' doing no work,' seems to have outgrown the Kindergarten. September 17 we moved from the Seegasse to the Reitbahngasse No. 20, into bright, sunny quarters. Moves are great events in children's lives : they like to help and to pack.

But when November came, still greater events were in store for you. Preparations were made for a journey to Vienna, on which Marie and Lieschen were to accompany us. At last, November 23, 6 A.M., we started, much to the children's delight. Julchen and the baby remained behind under Elwine's care.

The journey was a great amusement to the children. They were very sporting, and we were pleased with the way in which they adapted themselves to the less pleasant incidents of a journey. From Prague onwards we travelled by train ; they enjoyed this still more, and shortly before we reached Vienna Lieschen struck up with ' Comes a birdie a-flying,' with humorous variations. We arrived in Vienna on 27th. How many pages could I fill with our experiences there !

In later years remember particularly : The spire of St. Stephen's, the Bastion, the Pachers' house with Elise and her sister Emilie, where you enjoyed your delicious meals ; Fanny your maid, Ignatius our servant ; Herr Fischhof, Herr Likl, Herr Hanslick, who gave you presents ; finally, Mme. Lind, who took you upon her knees. She is a great singer, whose name you will often hear. I will also give you due praise for behaving well and keeping your place almost throughout, so that we were glad to have taken you with us.

You kept cheerful also on the journey back from Vienna, whence we started on January 21, 1847, in pretty severe weather ; amusing incidents were not wanting. Marie went to the theatre for the first time in Brünn, and again in Prague. You thoroughly enjoyed the good cooking at the Black Horse Hotel in Prague. But it would not do to live in such luxury all the year round ; therefore it was well that you returned to Dresden and regular habits on February 4.[1]

We found that Julchen, though still very delicate and

[1] The editor cannot refrain at this point from telling a favourite story which she has heard many times from Marie's lips. Papa's little girls, Marie, who was six, and Elise, four years and six months old, had very nearly lost themselves in the large town. ' Mamma was out,' Marie used to tell us, ' and Papa asked us whether we could remember the way to Dr. Fischhof's house. We confidently answered, " Yes ! " ' and he gave us a letter to take to this gentleman, whose quarters were in

weak, had made progress, but Emil was miserable and ailing. He does not yet take notice of anything, whines and grouses all day long, cannot be induced to smile, and no strengthening medicine seems to do him good.

Julchen is not unlike Marie in looks, but she is much quieter and more obstinate, and mentally backward by about a year compared with Marie at the age of two. Lieschen reminds me of my late mother, your grand-mother. Her humour and occasional sallies continue, also her spells of thoughtfulness and unreasonable fits of temper. But she often amuses us with her funny ideas, her resourceful wit and original appearance. Both returned fat and round from the journey.

Your parents' engagement to go to Berlin, where Papa was to conduct a performance of one of his works ('Peri'), compelled them to leave you for another six weeks. Marie had not wasted her time during their absence, and had started piano lessons with her aunt, Marie Wieck. We were pleased to hear her play five or six little exercises very nicely, still more to find her eager and industrious. Whenever she sees the piano open, she runs to it.

Lieschen is now beginning to knit.

On March 25 your parents returned from Berlin.

Count Baudissin and his wife often invited the children, and were particularly fond of Lieschen.

the same block of houses as ours, in the Grundlhof, but not quite easy to find. We became suddenly aware of having gone too far and arrived in St. Stephen's Square ; we looked about in consternation. We did not know how to get home, did not even remember the name of our street. We began to be frightened, for we had been told of the Bohemian rat-catchers who were on the look-out for little children. When our apprehension had reached its climax, we suddenly saw Mamma coming towards us like an angel from heaven. She was horrified to find us alone in the centre of the large town, took us home, and remonstrated with Papa. But he took it quite calmly, and said the children had assured him they knew the way.'

Grief when a good child tells a lie for the first time.

DRESDEN, 30 *June*.

Our little Emil died during the night 21-22 at 2.30 A.M. He was almost always ailing, has had few pleasures in this world. I have only once seen him smile ; that was when I took leave of him on the morning before we departed for Vienna. On Wednesday, June 23, at 6 P.M., he was buried.

You little ones do not yet realise your loss.

Since June 1, Emil and Julchen had been in the country, in Schärnitz, half an hour's distance from here. Julchen, who is still delicate, is benefited by the air and fresh milk. But it was not God's will that Emil should survive.

Julchen is still in Schärnitz with Elwine, and is to stay there during the summer.

Marie and Lieschen, you were healthy and often very high-spirited. Marie can now play twenty-two piano exercises ; on June 8, Papa's thirty-seventh birthday, she even played him one of his own little pieces, which goes like this :—

But Lieschen has no thought of doing lessons as yet ; some things, such as figures and letters, she picks up in play.

Your kind Mamma, who is already teaching you, Marie, the piano, also undertook to teach you reading and writing, and you have learnt a good deal with her. Nevertheless, you have not always been as industrious as you might have been. But you will no doubt improve, for you are always glad to do as your parents wish.

A cold which Marie has had lately has affected her ears, and she is a little deaf. But we are hoping it will soon pass.

Little Louise Viardot, the famous singer's daughter, was your playmate for a few days ; children could hardly be more different from each other than you and she, and the consequence was that you did not always agree. The little French girl, nevertheless, made an impression, especially on Marie.

We have taken you for many walks, almost every day. Once we were in Maxen with Marie.

Marie once said, ' God has made all things, men and animals and the whole world—and if there were no God, we should not even have a God.'

Since June 1 you have ceased to attend the Kindergarten, as you seemed to profit little by it on the whole, and it no longer even amused you.

DRESDEN, 21 *September.*

Since September 1, Julchen has been back from Schärnitz, and is already a great favourite with her parents. Her stay in the country has greatly benefited her, we should hardly have known her ; her mind particularly has developed ; she is very vivacious and sweet. But with her tiny, delicate physique she still looks more like a child of eighteen months.

Marie celebrated her sixth birthday very cheerfully. Gade from Leipzig arrived at the moment when she was given her presents.

Lieschen now does knitting every day. She seems very frightened at the prospect of school, while Marie was looking forward to it. Yesterday (Monday) was the great day on which she (Marie) went to a preparatory school for the first time, her slate under her arm, Waisenhaus Strasse 2 on the fourth floor, with Madame (name omitted). She returned in great spirits and said she would not mind going to school the whole day. I told her I would remind her of this in four weeks' time.

The children's chief amusement was a very simple swing in the arbour.

' Dominoes ' and ' Bell and Hammer ' are played with passionate enjoyment, especially by Marie.

Marie's progress in playing the piano is necessarily slow, for there are not many hours when she would not disturb Papa. She knows five scales (up to E major), and about twenty exercises.

DRESDEN, 28 *January* 1848.

Your lives, my dear children, have been untroubled by accidents or griefs since September. You are developing charmingly, and are the joy of your parents.

The world has sustained a great, irreparable loss during this time in the death on November 4 of Felix Mendelssohn. You, Mariechen, will be able later to appreciate this. He was your godfather, and you possess a beautiful silver cup with his name. You must value it greatly.

We spent Christmas very merrily.

On January 1 you started attending Dr. Frankenberg's Kindergarten again, for the school to which we had sent Marie did not seem very well managed, and things were expected of the children which their minds were unable to grasp.

On January 20, 1.45 A.M., a little brother was born to you, a strong, healthy child. Do not forget, Mariechen, how I fetched you from your bed in the night to show you the new arrival.

The piano lessons have come to an end for the present. Marie shows gifts and inclination for drawing as well. Her ear is getting more musical and true, too, as I notice with pleasure when she is singing her little songs.

Julchen is like a graceful little doll ; I have never known so charming and well-mannered a child.

Lieschen is growing fat and sturdy, a normal child. Marie remains slender.

May God bless and preserve you !

DRESDEN, 13 *October* 1848.

To our joy Ludwig is doing splendidly. Mamma says he ' will knock us all down in time.' He has a good wet-nurse. Julchen does not grow, she remains small and thin. But her mind is not as backward as her tiny physique would lead one to believe. She is obstinate, however, and takes no interest in her elder sisters' games.

Since October 1, Marie and Elise have been going to a proper school (Herr Mühl's). They are enjoying their lessons ; Marie especially is industrious, and good and obedient. They have also been attending Fräulein Malinska's piano school for the last six months, and are now playing all the scales and some little pieces. Papa made a present of some children's pieces to Marie for her birthday, which he greatly enjoyed writing.

You have been free from illnesses all this time ; we have every reason to be thankful for your preservation.

MEMOIRS OF EUGENIE SCHUMANN

Papa has made a long pause, for he had to write a great deal of music. Besides, these have been troubled times, the most revolutionary which the world has seen for centuries. You, dear children, have happily been preserved to us. Only, Marie was so ill during the last weeks of March that Mamma and Papa sat at her bedside in the saddest spirits imaginable. According to Dr. Helbig's diagnosis it was trouble in the parts round the heart. You were very slow in recovering, dear Marie—and when you were better, we were unspeakably relieved.

The most important event was our flight during the days of insurrection, May 5—a Saturday, when in our haste we seized you alone, Marie, by your hands, and rushed off with you, taking the train *via* Dohna to Maxen, to Major Serre's. On the following Monday Mamma fetched the others, as it was dangerous for men to go into the town. We stayed in Maxen till the Thursday. But on Friday we moved to Kreischa, and you will long remember this charming stay, which lasted nearly four weeks ; the beautiful trees and fields, springs and fountains, the cuckoo, the lilies-of-the-valley, the ' Herr Baron's ' children. Julchen especially has been benefited by the country air, although she still does not grow.

We sent you to the village school in Kreischa, so that you should not be quite idle, and I am glad to be able to say of you elder ones, Marie and Elise, that you seem to like lessons and instruction, and are giving satisfaction to your parents.

On July 12 we returned to Dresden.

Marie's musical talent is becoming more and more evident ; she shows keenness, inclination, a good ear, an excellent memory, and is beginning to sing little inventions of her own, *e.g.* melodies fitted to nursery rhymes. Unfortunately there is little time for her practising, but we must see to that.

Lieschen too shows a liking for music. Ludwig burbles. Julchen often shows signs of a keen intelligence, side by side with greediness. She often says the most amusing things. She has been going to Dr. Frankenberg's Kindergarten for the last few months ; the elder ones are going to Herr Mühl's preparatory school and Fräulein Malinska's school of pianoforte playing. God bless you !

The death of a kind brother of your Papa's (April 9) —your uncle—occurred during this time. He has often taken Marie and Lieschen on his knees. While we were in Russia, you were living for a whole winter in Schneeberg with him.

Now you have only a great-uncle (in Greiz), a cousin (Richard S. in Gleichen) ; also four girl cousins, the two daughters of Karl Sch., Rosalie and Anna, and two of Julius Sch., Emilie and Mathilde Schumann. But these are the relations on Papa's side only.

5 *July*.

Yesterday a little story with a moral occurred to me :

Let every one keep to his element.

The fishes became bored at last with being for ever in the water. ' Why ! ' they said, ' outside everything looks nice and green, the sun is shining brightly, but we lose all this, here in the water.' Then they made a conspiracy to drink the whole pond dry. So they began, and drank and drank till the water got lower and lower. Their joy reached its summit when they felt themselves on dry land and the hot sun shone upon them. But it did not last long—they became feebler and more lifeless from minute to minute ; there was not a drop of water left to quench their thirst, and they died a miserable death. Let every one keep to his element.

Quotations from E. M. Arndt :—

If you would be happy, pray daily to your God, your beauty, and your love.

Daily crush your ambitions and pride if you would become a glad and strong warrior.

You need only be courageous and abandon care for the morrow to win through gloriously : *serenity !*

Riches and strength lift up the heart, but the fear of the Lord is above them both.—ECCLESIASTICUS.

On the last page but one of the Little Book of Memories are the entries :—

Paul Ferdinand, born in Dresden, July 16, 1849, 1.30 P.M.; christened September 25. Godparents : Frau Oberländer, wife of the Minister Oberländer ; Herr Felix Güntz, barrister ; and Herr Franz Schubert, first violinist, of Dresden.

Eugenie, born in Düsseldorf, December 1, 1851, in the first hour of the day (a minute before 1) ; christened January 31, 1852. Godparents : Frau Hasenclever, *née* Schadow, wife of Dr. Hasenclever ; Fräulein Leser ; Professor Theodor Hildebrandt ; and Dr. Wolfgang Müller.

On the last page is the entry :—

One of the first to celebrate Holy Communion according to the Lutheran rites (1531-32), at the Court of Henry the Pious in Freiberg, was a clergyman of the name of Schumann.

See Böttger's *History of Saxony.*

Printed in Great Britain by T. and A. CONSTABLE LTD.
at the University Press, Edinburgh